Series / Number 07-049

# BASIC
# CONTENT
# ANALYSIS

**ROBERT PHILIP WEBER**
*Harvard University*

**SAGE PUBLICATIONS**
Beverly Hills   London   New Delhi

*For information address:*

SAGE Publications, Inc.
275 South Beverly Drive
Beverly Hills, California 90212

SAGE Publications India Pvt. Ltd.
M-32 Market
Greater Kailash I
New Delhi 110 048, India

SAGE Publications Ltd
28 Banner Street
London EC1Y 8QE
England

International Standard Book Number 0-8039-2448-8

Library of Congress Catalog Card No. 85-050051

FIRST PRINTING

When citing a professional paper, please use the proper form. Remember to cite the
correct Sage University Paper series title and include the paper number. One of the
following formats can be adapted (depending on the style manual used):

(1) IVERSEN, GUDMUND R. and NORPOTH, HELMUT (1976) "Analysis of
Variance." Sage University Paper series on Quantitative Applications in the Social
Sciences, 07-001. Beverly Hills and London: Sage Pubns.

*OR*

(2) Iversen, Gudmund R. and Norpoth, Helmut. 1976. *Analysis of Variance.* Sage
University Paper series on Quantitative Applications in the Social Sciences, series no.
07-001. Beverly Hills and London: Sage Pubns.

# CONTENTS

## Series Editor's Introduction

Communication is at the heart of social interaction. For the many social scientists interested in analyzing communication, there is no lack of pertinent data. Documents of various kinds exist over long periods of time—often centuries—spanning periods for which other kinds of empirical evidence are almost totally lacking. The sources of relevant texts are numerous, including books, magazines, newspapers, transcripts of speeches, conversations, radio and television programs, and interviews. The difficulty for the research is therefore not the availability of data but the need for appropriate means of analyzing it.

*Basic Content Analysis,* by Robert Philip Weber, is a concise introduction to text analysis for both novices and more experienced researchers. The basic idea is to classify the words of the text into content categories. Because a major concern in content analysis is with the quality of the categorization, Chapter 2 discusses at length aspects of the classification process that affect the reliability and validity of the resulting content variables. A step-by-step procedure for developing, testing, and applying a set of content categories is also presented. This chapter also discusses several problems that arise in the construction of category schemes, as well as the relative merits of proposed solutions.

As Weber notes, content analysis is a set of techniques for text analysis that investigators can readily use. The goals of the research must determine the selection of a particular technique. Chapter 3 shows in detail several ways of analyzing texts that have proven useful in the past. These techniques range from simple tabular methods of organizing and displaying text to multivariate statistical procedures. More advanced, technical matters are handled by endnotes and references to the literature, creating a highly readable presentation.

The concluding chapter addresses unresolved problems in content analysis and shows an interesting example of an experimental artificial intelligence system for text understanding. Weber suggests that in the next 3 to 5 years these systems will become more important for content analysis.

In short, *Basic Content Analysis* is an important new guide to text analysis that will be useful to students, faculty, and researchers in the social sciences.

—*Richard G. Niemi*
Series Co-Editor

## Acknowledgments

This research was supported in part by ZUMA, the Center for Surveys, Methods, and Analysis, Mannheim, FRG. I remain indebted to the generosity of past and present directors and staff, especially Hans-Dieter Klingemann, Peter Philip Mohler, Karl Ulrich Mayer, Max Kaase, and Manfred Keuchler. Additional support was provided by Kurzweil Computer Products, Inc., a subsidiary of Xerox Corp. Sue Williamson of Kurzweil played a key role, and her generosity and help is gratefully acknowledged. Randi Lynn Miller assisted with data entry at an earlier phase of the research. Thanks to Nancy Marshall, J. Zvi Namenwirth, Barbara Norman, Philip J. Stone, Kathrine Tenerowicz, and two anonymous reviewers for detailed comments on earlier drafts. Thanks also to the Harvard University Computing Center for computer resources. Thanks to Zvi Namenwirth for permission to quote extensively from Namenwirth and Bibbee (1975); to Dexter Dunphy for permission to reproduce a figure from Dunphy, et al., 1974; to Human Sciences Press for permission to adapt or reprint some material from Weber (1984b); to Elsevier Publishing Company for permission to adapt or reprint some material from Weber (1983); and to the Austrian Academy of Sciences for permission to adapt or reprint some material that appeared in Weber (1984a). Thanks also to the MIT Press, for permission to excerpt *In-Depth Understanding: A Computer Model of Integrated Processing of Narrative Comprehension,* © Michael G. Dyer and the Massachusetts Institute of Technology (Cambridge: MIT Press, 1983).

# BASIC CONTENT ANALYSIS

## ROBERT PHILIP WEBER
*Harvard University*

## 1. INTRODUCTION

**Content analysis is a research** methodology that utilizes a set of procedures to make valid inferences from text.[1] These inferences are about the sender(s) of message, the message itself, or the audience of the message. The rules of this inferential process vary with the theoretical and substantive interests of the investigator, and are discussed in subsequent chapters.

Content analysis can be used for many purposes. The following list points out a few notable examples (adapted from Berelson, 1952):

- disclose international differences in communication content
- compare media or "levels" of communication
- audit communication content against objectives
- code open-ended questions in surveys
- identify the intentions and other characteristics of the communicator
- determine the psychological state of persons or groups
- detect the existence of propaganda
- describe attitudinal and behavioral responses to communications
- reflect cultural patterns of groups, institutions, or societies
- reveal the focus of individual, group, institutional, or societal attention
- describe trends in communication content

The numerous examples presented throughout this book mainly illustrate the last three uses of content analysis.

This monograph is an introduction to content analysis methodology from a social science perspective.[2] The material covered here will be useful to students and researchers who wish to analyze text. The following chapters assume that the reader has had at least introductory courses in research methods and in data analysis or social statistics.

One important use of content analysis is the generation of culture indicators that point to the state of beliefs, values, ideologies, or other culture systems (Melischek et al., 1984; Rosengren, 1981; Namenwirth, 1969b, 1973, 1984a; Namenwirth and Lasswell, 1970; Weber, 1981, 1982, 1984a; Weber and Namenwirth, 1984; Klingemann et al., 1982). Based on political documents and other texts, culture indicator research determines how the concerns of a single society, institution, group, or other social organization differ. Many studies are comparative and examine the similarities and differences in the concerns of more than one society or group. Other investigations contrast the concerns of two or more social units through time.

Compared with other data-generating and analysis techniques, content analysis has several advantages:

- Communications is a central aspect of social interaction. Content analytic procedures operate directly upon text or transcripts of human communications.

- The best content analytic studies utilize both qualitative and quantitative operations on texts. Thus, content analysis methodology combines what are usually thought to be antithetical modes of analysis.

- Documents of various kinds exist over long periods of time. Culture indicators generated from such series of documents constitute reliable data that may span even centuries (e.g., Weber, 1981, 1982; Namenwirth, 1973).

- In more recent times, when reliable data of other kinds exist, culture indicators can be used to assess quantitatively the relationships among economic, social, political, and cultural change.

- Compared with techniques such as interviews, content analysis usually yields unobtrusive measures in which neither the sender nor the receiver of the message is aware that it is being analyzed. Hence, there is little danger that the act of measurement itself will act as a force for change that confounds the data (Webb et al., 1966).

Two very different studies summarized below illustrate some ways content analysis has been used. Subsequent chapters explain other studies in great detail.

## Some Content-Analytic Studies

Content analysis has been used to study popular art forms. Walker (1975) analyzed differences and similarities in American Black and White popular song lyrics, 1962-1973. Using computer-aided content analysis, Walker investigated differences in narrative form. He found that compared to popular (White) song lyrics, rhythm and blues and soul song lyrics show greater emphasis on action in the objective world, less concern with time, and greater emphasis on what Walker calls "toughmindedness" or "existential concreteness."

The study also investigated changes in narrative focus. Walker (1975) found that identification with others increased significantly over time in soul and rhythm and blues lyrics, but not in popular song lyrics. This change may reflect increasing self-awareness and positive images within the Black community.

Walker's study illustrates that computer-based content analysis may be used to study popular as well as elite culture. In fact, one important substantive question content analysis might address is the relationship between popular and elite culture. Specifically, do changes in elite culture lead or lag behind changes in mass culture? Unfortunately, one serious difficulty exists in any study addressing this question: Textual materials that survive over long periods often reflect an elite bias.

In another study, Aries (1973; summarized in Aries, 1977), also using computer-aided content analysis, studied differences in female, male and mixed-sex small groups. She found that differential sex-role socialization and sex-role stereotyping affect thematic content and social interaction. In female groups, women indicate a great deal of concern with interpersonal issues. Women discuss "themselves, their homes and families, and their relationships, defining themselves by the way they relate to significant others who surround them" (Aries, 1973: 254).

In male groups, members do not directly address interpersonal matters. Instead, men indirectly relate personal experiences and feelings in the form of stories and metaphor. Men "achieve a closeness through the sharing of laughter and stories of activities, rather than the sharing of the understanding of those experiences" (Aries, 1973: 254). In addition, all-male group manifest more themes involving aggression than do all-female groups.

In mixed groups, Aries found that women talked less of their homes and families. Women also spoke less of achievement and institutions. In short, women in these groups "orient themselves around being women with men by assuming the traditional female role" (Aries, 1973: 256).

Men in mixed groups expressed their competitiveness less through story-telling than through assuming leadership roles in the group. Moreover, in the presence of women, men shift more towards reflection of themselves and their feelings.

Aries's study illustrates that content analysis may be:

- applied to substantive problems at the intersection of culture, social structure, and social interaction;
- used to generate dependent variables in experimental designs; and
- used to study small groups as microcosms of society.

Changes in sex-role socialization could be assessed by repeating the study. Furthermore, Aries's research could be extended with appropriate modifications to cross-national and cross-language research designs.

## Issues in Content Analysis

A central idea in content analysis is that the many words of the text are classified into much fewer content categories. Each category may consist of one, several, or many words. Words, phrases, or other units of text classified in the same category are presumed to have similar meanings.[3] Depending upon the purposes of the investigator, this similarity may be based on the precise meaning of the words, such as grouping synonyms together, or may be based on words sharing similar connotations, such as grouping together several words implying a concern with a category like Wealth[4] or Power.

In order to draw valid inferences from the text, it is important that the classification procedure used be reliable in the sense of being consistent: Different people should code the same text in the same way. In addition, the classification procedure must generate variables that are valid. A variable is valid to the extent that it measures or represents what the investigator intends it to measure. Because of the central importance of such factors, the second chapter discusses reliability, validity, and content classification in detail.

In the past, investigators have employed a variety of methods to draw inferences from text. The third chapter presents a wide range of techniques that have proved useful.[5] Some of these methods are quite simple, and, in a sense, linguistically naive.[6] However, one should not make the mistake of believing, as some do, that naive procedures must be put to naive uses. Many of these simple techniques produce highly reliable and valid indicators of symbolic content. Other content-analytic techniques are more complex or can be used in conjunction with statistical methods. Chapter 3 explains the use of these techniques, but highly technical matters are handled by footnotes or references to the literature.

Because of the proliferation of computers generally and the growing capacities of microcomputers, Chapter 3 focuses on computer-aided content analysis. Computers can be used to easily manipulate the text, displaying it in various ways that often reveal aspects of symbol usage not otherwise apparent. For example, one can display all sentences or other units of texts containing a particular word or phrase. Another use of computers is to count symbols, such as all occurrences of the phrase "United States."

Although this monograph presents numerous examples of what was put into and produced by a computer, it does not specify the instructions given the computer (i.e., the computer programs). However, the Appendix discusses several programs for text analysis, and includes information on hardware compatibility and sofware sources. The Appendix also provides some information on publicly available text data bases that are in machine-readable form.

The fourth and concluding chapter looks to the future. After reviewing some currently unresolved problems in content analysis, it presents an example illustrating recent advances in the field of artificial intelligence and discusses some implications for social science inquiry.

**Concluding Remarks**

The spirit of the following material is illustrative and didactic rather than dogmatic. There is no simple *right way* to do content analysis. Instead, each investigator must judge what methods are appropriate for her or his substantive problem. Moreover, some technical problems in content analysis have yet to be resolved or are the subject of on-going research and debate. Where possible, this book tries to state the problem clearly, to indicate alternative resolutions, if they are known, and to suggest what kinds of information or capabilities might help resolve the matter.

Rather than presenting an exegesis of the existing literature, this work deliberately emphasizes material not covered or stressed elsewhere. The goal is to produce a more interesting and useful book for those contemplating or actually doing research using content analysis. During the past 10 years, the introduction of relatively inexpensive microcomputers, the introduction of cost-effective devices for making text machine-readable, and the the reduction of computer costs generally, have renewed interest in content analysis. Certainly, these tools will be increasingly applied to a wide range of social science questions during the next few years.

As a brief introduction to content analysis, much is omitted. Consequently, there are suggestions for further reading at the end of each chapter. These books and articles address content analysis methods, substantive research, general issues in research methodology, or statistics at a much greater level of detail than is possible or even desirable here.

**Suggestions for Further Reading**

There are several books on content analysis that should be read by anyone seriously interested in the subject. Krippendorff (1980) is a good recent survey of the field and its problems. It is especially useful for those doing human-coded content analysis. His discussion of reliability is "must" reading. However, the book is not up-to-date regarding the use of computers.

Other books contain numerous methodological insights and practical information. One is the book on the General Inquirer system (Stone et al., 1966), the first widely used computer system for content analysis. Although the version discussed there is not the current one (see Kelly and Stone, 1975), this book presents a wide-ranging discussion of content analysis, its problems, and practical solutions. Stone and his associates also present several chapters illustrating the application of computer-aided content analysis to a variety of substantive problems. Another useful resource is a set of conference papers edited by Gerbner et al. (1969). This interdisciplinary collection addresses many issues still current in content analysis. In addition, Holsti's (1969) brief discussion is worthwhile reading. North et al. (1963) apply a variety of content-analytic techniques to the study of communications in international relations. Finally, there is an earlier, precomputer body of work on (or using) content analysis—notably, Berelson (1952), Lasswell, Leites et al. (1965), Lasswell et al. (1952), and Pool (1952, 1959).

## 2. CONTENT CLASSIFICATION AND INTERPRETATION

The central problems of content analysis originate mainly in the data-reduction process by which the many words of texts are classified into much fewer content categories. One set of problems concerns the consistency or reliability of text classification. In context analysis, reliability problems usually grow out of the ambiguity of word meanings or the ambiguity of category definitions or other coding rules. Classification by multiple human coders permits the quantitative assessment of achieved reliability. Classification by computer, however, leads to perfect coder reliability (under the assumptions of correct computer programs and well-functioning computer hardware). Once properly defined for the computer, the coding rules are always applied in the same way.

A much more difficult set of problems concerns the validity of variables based on content classification. A content analysis variable is valid to the extent that it measures the construct the investigator intends it to measure. As is the case with reliability, validity problems also grow out of the ambiguity of word meanings and category or variable definitions.

As an introduction to these problems, consider two sample texts and some simple coding rules. Using common sense definitions, imagine that the coding instructions define five categories: Citizens' Rights, Economic, Government, Political Doctrine, and Welfare. Imagine also that coders are instructed to classify each whole paragraph in one and only one category. Consider first a portion of the Carter 1980 Democratic platform:

Our current economic situation is unique. In 1977, we inherited a severe recession from the Republicans. The Democratic Administration and the Democratic Congress acted quickly to reduce the unacceptably high levels of unemployment and to stimulate the economy. And we succeeded. We recovered from that deep recession and our economy was strengthened and revitalized. As that fight was won, the enormous increases in foreign oil prices—120 percent last year—and declining productivity fueled an inflationary spiral that also had to be fought. The Democrats did that, and inflation has begun to recede. In working to combat these dual problems, significant economic actions have been taken [Johnson, 1982: 38].

Now consider another paragraph from the Reagan 1980 Republican platform:

> Through long association with government programs, the word "welfare" has come to be perceived almost exclusively as tax-supported aid to the needy. But in its most inclusive sense—and as Americans understood it from the beginning of the Republic—such aid also encompasses those charitable works performed by private citizens, families, and social, ethnic, and religious organizations. Policies of the federal government leading to high taxes, rising inflation, and bureaucratic empire-building have made it difficult and often impossible for such individuals and groups to exercise their charitable instincts. We believe that government policies that fight inflation, reduce tax rates, and end bureaucratic excesses can help make private effort by the American people once again a major force in those works of charity which are the true signs of a progressive and humane society [Johnson, 1982: 179].

Most people would code the first excerpt in the Economic category, but the proper coding of the second is less obvious. This paragraph could be taken to be mainly about the rights of citizens, or about the desirability of restricting the government's role, the welfare state, or to be the espousal of a political doctrine. In fact, it occurs at the end of a section titled *Improving the Welfare System.*

The difficulty of classifying the second excerpt is partly contrived by the present author, as it results from the lack of clear and detailed coding rules for each category and from the variety of subject matter. Large portions of text, such as paragraphs and whole texts, are usually more difficult to code as a unit than smaller portions, such as words and phrases, because large units typically contain more information and greater diversity of topics. Hence they are more likely to present coders with conflicting cues.

These examples illustrate the kind of problems investigators face when coding text. The next two sections look more systematically at coding problems from the perspectives of reliability and validity assessment, respectively.

### Reliability

Three types of reliability are pertinent to content analysis; *stability, reproducibility,* and *accuracy* (Krippendorff, 1980: 130-154).

Stability refers to the extent to which the results of content classification are invariant over time. Stability can be ascertained when the same content is coded more than once by the *same coder*. Inconsistencies in coding constitute unreliability. These inconsistencies may stem from a variety of factors, including ambiguities in the coding rules, ambiguities in the text, cognitive changes within the coder, or simple errors, such as recording the wrong numeric code for a category. Because only one person is coding, stability is the weakest form of reliability.

Reproducibility, sometimes called *intercoder reliability,* refers to the extent to which content classification produces the same results when the same text is coded by *more than one coder*. Conflicting codings usually result from cognitive differences among the coders, ambiguous coding instructions, or from random recording errors. High reproducibility is a minimum standard for content analysis. This is because stability measures the consistency of private understandings, whereas reproducibility measures the consistency of shared understandings, or meanings.

Accuracy refers to the extent to which the classification of text corresponds to a standard or norm. It is the strongest form of reliability. As Krippendorff notes (1980: 131), it has sometimes been used to test the performance of human coders when a standard coding for some text has already been established. Except for training purposes, standard codings are infrequently established for texts. Consequently, researchers seldom use accuracy in reliability assessment.

Krippendorff (1980: 132) also points out that many investigators fail totally to assess the reliability of their coding. Even when reliability is assessed, some investigators engage in practices that often make data seem more reliable than they actually are. In particular, when coders have disagreed, investigators have resolved these disagreements by negotiations or by invoking the authority of the principal investigator or senior graduate assistant. Resolving these disagreements may produce judgments biased toward the opinions of the most verbal or more senior of the coders. Consequently, the reliability of the coding should be calculated *before* these disagreements are resolved. Krippendorff goes on to illustrate several ways of calculating reliabilities for human coders. Readers who plan to do human-coded content analysis should pay close attention to Krippendorff's discussion. Subsequent sections of this chapter return to reliability issues in conjunction with category construction and word classification.

**Validity**

The term *validity* is potentially confusing because it has been used in a variety of ways in the methodology literature (compare Brinberg and Kidder, 1982; Cook and Campbell, 1979; Campbell and Stanley, 1963). However, two distinctions may help clarify the concept. The first is between validity as correspondence between two sets of things, such as concepts, variables, methods, and data, and validity as generalizability of results, inferences, and theory (Brinberg and McGrath, 1982). For example, if the same construct is measured by two different methods, and the resulting variables are highly correlated, then these variables are valid indicators of the construct.[7] These results would also indicate that the concept can be generalized in the sense that its measurement is not dependent upon a particular operation. Imagine, for example, two categories indicating concern with Hostility—one based on classifying words, the other based on classifying sentences. Imagine further that for the same set of texts, these different measures are highly correlated. This finding would indicate that both variables measure the same construct, and thus are both valid indicators.

Furthermore, if results from a number of studies agree, this correspondence suggests that the results are valid because they can be generalized from a variety of research situations. Correspondence and generalizability are essential aspects of the several types of validity discussed in this chapter.

A second distinction, more specific to content analysis, is between the validity of the classification scheme or variables derived from it, and the validity of the interpretation relating content variables to their causes or consequences. To assert that a category or variable (Economic, for example) is valid is to assert that there is a correspondence between the category and the abstract concept that it represents (concern with economic matters). To assert that a research result based on content analysis is valid is to assert that the finding does not depend upon, or is generalizable beyond the specific data, methods, or measurements of a particular study. For instance, if a computer-assisted content analysis of party platforms indicates a strong relationship between long-term economic fluctuations and concern with the well-being of economy and society, then the validity of the results would increase to the extent that other data (e.g., newspaper editorials), other coding procedures (e.g., human rather than computer-coded), or other classification schemes (dictionaries) produced similar substantive conclusions.

Perhaps the weakest form of validity is *face* validity, which is based on the correspondence between the investigator's definition of a concept and her or his definition of the category that measures it. A category has face validity to the extent that it appears to measure the construct it is intended to measure. Even if a number of expert judges agree, face validity is still a weak claim as it rests on a single variable. Stronger forms of validity involve more than one variable. Unfortunately, content analysts tend to rely heavily on face validity; consequently, other social scientists often view their results with some skepticism.

Much stronger validity is obtained by comparing content-analytic data with some external criterion. Four types of external validity are pertinent.

A measure has *construct validity*[8] to the extent that it is correlated with some other measure of the same construct. Campbell and Fiske (1959) and others (e.g., Alwin, 1974; Althauser, 1974; Fiske, 1982; Campbell and O'Connell, 1982) further differentiate *convergent* from *discriminant* validity. A measure has high construct validity when it correlates with other measures of the same construct (convergent) and is uncorrelated with measures of dissimilar constructs (discriminant). Construct validity entails the generalizability of the construct across measures or methods.

The research reported in Saris-Gallhofer et al. (1978) is a fine example of applying these ideas to content-analytic data. The object of this study was to validate a content analysis dictionary developed by Holsti (1969) using the main categories of the Semantic Differential (Osgood et al., 1957; Snider and Osgood, 1969; Osgood et al., 1975; Anderson, 1970). The Semantic Differential is a technique for assessing the primary categories people use in affective evaluation or classification. The details of the technique are not pertinent here. However, research in a variety of cultures indicates that people use three basic dimensions of classification. Each dimension is anchored by polar opposites:

- Evaluation: positive versus negative affect;
- Potency: strength versus weakness; and,
- Activity: active versus passive.

Each word in Holsti's (1969) dictionary was assigned a number representing the extent to which it indicates each dimension of the semantic differential. Saris-Gallhofer and her colleagues (1978) compared Holsti's assignment of scores with Osgood's and with scores assigned by a group of students. Thus, each word (or other unit of text) was classified by three different methods. Each method claims to classify text on the same constructs. Using statistical techniques designed to assess convergent and discriminant validity, Saris-Gallhofer found that Holsti's scoring for the Evaluation and Potency dimensions was much more valid than his scoring for the Activity dimension. It remains unclear why Holsti's scoring of the Activity dimension is less valid than the scoring for the other two. Additional research is required to determine the specific factors that affect the validity of content classification. Nonetheless, this study shows that sophisticated statistical techniques useful in assessing validity can be applied to content analysis data.

*Hypothesis validity,* the second type of validity, relies on the correspondence among variables and the correspondence between these relationships and theory. A measure has hypothesis validity if in relationship to other variables it "behaves" as it is expected to.[9] For example, several studies based on political documents, such as party platforms in presidential campaigns, have shown that the preoccupation of society with economic issues increases during bad economic times and decreases when the economy is good (e.g., Namenwirth, 1969b, 1973; Weber, 1982, 1984a). These results are consistent with theoretical arguments relating the cultural and social processes that generate political documents (such as party platforms) with changes in the economy. Thus, the observed inverse relationship between economic fluctuations and concern with economic matters indicates the hypothesis validity of measured variables and the constructs they represent.

A measure has *predictive validity,* the third type, to the extent that forecasts about events or conditions external to the study are shown to correspond to actual events or conditions. These predictions may concern either future, past (postdiction), or concurrent events. Predictive validity is powerful because the inferences from data are successfully generalized beyond the study to situations not under the direct control of the investigator.

Content-analytic data are seldom shown to have predictive validity,[10] but three examples illustrate the point.

- Ogilvie et al. (1966) analyzed real suicide notes from 33 males who had been matched for age, gender, occupation, religion, and ethnicity with 33 nonsuicidal controls who were asked to produce simulated suicide notes. Using General Inquirer type computer-aided content analysis, Stone was able to correctly distinguish real from simulated suicide notes in 30 of the 33 pairs (90.9%) of notes.

- George (1959a) studied inferences made by The Foreign Broadcast Intelligence Service of the F.C.C. from German propaganda during World War II. He found that Allied intelligence analysts often could anticipate changes in German war tactics and strategy from changes in the content of radio broadcasts and other media.

- Namenwirth's (1973) analysis of party platforms in presidential campaigns, written in the late 1960s, suggested that America would experience severe economic difficulties that would peak about 1980. Events since seem to confirm this prediction.

Words or other coding units classified together need to possess similar connotations in order for the classification to have *semantic validity,* the fourth and final type of validity. According to Krippendorff (1980: 159ff), semantic validity exists when persons familiar with the language and texts examine lists of words (or other units) placed in the same category and agree that these words have similar meanings or connotations.

Although this seems to be an obvious requirement for valid content analysis, many difficulties arise because of the ambiguities of words and of category definitions. For example, the early systems for computer-aided content analysis could not distinguish between the various senses of words with more than one meaning, such as "mine." Does this refer to a hole in the ground, the process of extraction, or a possessive pronoun? Because of this failure, word counts including the frequency of "mine" lacked semantic validity. Various aspects of semantic validity are discussed later in this and in subsequent chapters.

## Creating and Testing a Coding Scheme

Many studies require the investigator to design and implement a coding scheme. Whether the coding is to be done by humans or computer, the process of creating and applying a coding scheme includes several basic steps. Assuming that the investigator has identified the substantive questions to be investigated, relevant theories, previous research, and the text to be classified, he or she next proceeds with the following necessary steps:

(1) *Define the recording units.* One of the most fundamental and important decisions concerns the definition of the basic unit of text to be classified. There are six common options:

- Word—One choice is to code each word. As noted, early computer software for text analysis did not have the ability to distinguish among the various senses of words with more than one meaning, and hence produced ambiguous results.

- Word Sense—More recent computer programs have the ability to code the different senses of words with multiple meanings and to code phrases that constitute a semantic unit, such as idioms (e.g., "taken for granted") or proper nouns (e.g., "the Empire State Building"). These issues are discussed in detail later in this chapter.

- Sentence—An entire sentence is often the recording unit when the investigator is interested in words or phrases that occur together. For example, coders may be instructed to count sentences in which either positive, negative, or affectively neutral references are made to the Soviet Union. A sentence with the phrase "evil empire" would be counted as Negative Evaluation; "Talks with the Soviet Union continue," would be coded Neutral Evaluation.

- Theme—Holsti (1963: 136, emphasis in the original) defines a theme as a unit of text "having *no more than one each of the following elements:* (1) the *perceiver,* (2) the *perceived,* or agent of action, (3) the *action,* (4) the *target* of the action." For example, the sentence "The President / hates / Communists" would be divided as shown. Numeric or other codes are often inserted in the text to represent subject / verb / object. This form of coding preserves important information and provides a means of distinguishing between the sentence above and the assertion that "Communists hate the President."
  Sometimes long, complex sentences must be broken down into theme format. Parts of speech shared between themes must be repeated. In addition, ambiguous phrases and pronouns must be identified manually. These steps are taken prior to coding for the content. Holsti (1963: 136-137) gives the following example of

editing more complex sentences before coding for themes and content:[11]

> [T]he sentence, "The American imperialists have perverted the peace and are preparing to attack the Socialist Camp," must be edited to read: "The American imperialists have perverted the peace + (the Americans) are preparing to attack the Socialist Camp."

This form of coding is labor intensive, but leads to much more detailed and sophisticated comparisons. See Holsti (1963, 1966, 1969) for further details.

- Paragraph—When computer assistance is not feasible and when resources for human codings are limited, investigators sometimes code whole paragraphs in order to reduce the effort required. Evidence discussed later in this chapter indicates that it is more difficult to achieve high reliability when coding large units, such as paragraphs, than when coding smaller units, such as words.

- Whole text—Unless the whole text is relatively short, like newspaper headlines, editorials, or stories, it is difficult to achieve high reliability when coding whole texts.

(2) *Define the categories.* In creating category definitions, investigators must make two basic decisions. (Other related issues are taken up later.) The first is whether or not the categories are to be mutually exclusive. Most statistical procedures require variables that are not confounded. If a recording unit can be classified simultaneously in two or more categories and if both categories (variables) are included in the same statistical analysis, then it is possible that the basic statistical assumptions of the analysis are violated and the results dubious.

The second choice concerns how narrow or broad the categories are to be. Some categories are limited because of language. For example, a category indicating self-references defined as first person singular pronouns will have only a few words or entries. A category defined as Concern with Economic matters may have many entries. For some purposes, however, it may make sense to use much more narrow or specific categories, such as Inflation, Taxes, Budget, Trade, Agriculture, and so on.

(3) *Test coding on sample of text.* The best test of the clarity of category definitions is to code a small sample of the text. Testing not

only reveal ambiguities in the rules, but it often leads to insights suggesting revisions of the classification scheme.

(4) *Assess accuracy or reliability.* Accuracy in this sense means the text is correctly coded by the computer, not in the sense of a type of reliability that was discussed earlier. If human coders are used, the reliability of the coding process should be estimated *before* resolving disputes among the coders.

(5) *Revise coding rules.* If the reliability is low, or if errors in computer procedures are discovered, the coding rules must be revised.

(6) *Return to step 3.* This cycle will continue until the coders achieve sufficient reliability or until the computer procedures work correctly.

(7) *Code all the text.* When high coder reliability has been achieved or when the computer programs are functioning correctly, the coding rules can then be applied to all the text.

(8) *Assess achieved reliability or accuracy.* The reliability of human coders should be assessed after the text is classified. Never assume that if samples of text were reliably coded, then the whole corpus of text will also be reliably coded. Human coders are subject to fatigue and are likely to make more mistakes as the coding continues. Their understanding of the coding rules may change in subtle ways as the text is coded, and this leads to unreliability.

If the coding was done by computer, the output should be carefully checked to insure that the coding rules were correctly applied. Text not in the sample(s) used for testing may present novel combinations of words that were not anticipated or encountered earlier, and these may cause errors in classification.

## Dictionaries and Computerized
## Text Classification

Content analysts have used several strategies to create categories and variables. Some investigators have counted by hand a few key words or phrases. Tufte (1978: 75), for example, counted certain words in the 1976 Democratic and Republican party platforms, including indicators of distributional issues, such as "inequity," "regressive," "equal," and "redistribution," and indicators of concern with inflation, such as "inflation," "inflationary," "price stability," and "rising prices."

Others have constructed a set of content categories based on a single concept. For example, the early version of Stone's General Inquirer computer system was used to analyze achievement imagery (McClelland's N-Achievement; Stone et al., 1966: 191ff). This approach offers several advantages. It permits the intensive and detailed analysis of a single theoretical construct. It also provides an explicit rationale not only for what is retained, but also for what is excluded from the analysis. Furthermore, single-concept coding schemes often have high validity and reliability.

Another approach to content analysis involves the creation and application of general dictionaries.[12] Content analysis dictionaries consist of category names, the definitions or rules for assigning words to categories, and the actual assignment of specific words. This strategy provides the researcher with numerous categories (60 to 150+) into which most words in most texts can be classified.[13] Once created, general dictionaries are advantageous because they:

- provide a wide range of categories to chose from (see, for example, Stone et al., 1966: 42-44);

- minimize the time needed for dictionary construction, validation, and revision;

- standardize classification; and

- encourage the accumulation of comparable results when used in many studies.[14]

It is worth noting here that dictionary construction is commonly misperceived to be merely a preface or preparatory step for quantification. Although researchers commonly use dictionaries to define variables for quantification, they also employ categories to locate and retrieve text based on the occurrence of semantically equivalent symbols. Chapter 3 presents examples of retrievals based on categories.

Certain problems arise in the creation of *any* content category or set of categories. These problems stem from the ambiguity of both the category definitions and of the words that are to be assigned to categories. To facilitate discussion of these difficulties, two general dictionaries are used as examples, the Harvard IV Psychosocial Dictionary, developed by Dexter Dunphy and his associates (Dunphy et al., 1974; Kelly and Stone, 1975), and the Lasswell Value Dictionary

(LVD), developed and extended by J. Zvi Namenwirth and his associates (Lasswell and Namenwirth, 1968; Namenwirth and Weber, 1984). Both dictionaries are used in conjunction with Stone's General Inquirer system for the analysis of English language text.[15]

Tables 2.1 and 2.2 present definitions of selected content categories from the LVD and Harvard IV dictionaries, respectively.[16] Categories are often represented by abbreviations or tags that appear in these tables. The process of classifying words in texts is known as *tagging*. The categories that appear in these tables illustrate similarities and differences between the dictionaries and introduce the analysis of sample text presented below and in Chapter 3.

One set of LVD categories contains those words, word senses,[17] and idioms that denote wealth-related matters. Another category contains wealth words indicating a transaction or exchange of value (Wealth-Transactions), such as forms of the verbs "buy," "sell," and "mortgage." A third category contains words that name a role or person involved in wealth matters (Wealth-Participants), such as "banker," "buyer," and "seller."

As noted, the construction of valid and useful content categories depends upon the interaction between language and the classification scheme (Namenwirth and Weber, 1984). For example, one can often think of categories for which only a few words exist, such as a category for first person singular pronouns (e.g., Self in the LVD). To avoid difficulties[18] stemming from categories with limited numbers of words, the LVD aggregates the remaining wealth-related words, word senses, and idioms indicating a concern with wealth into a Wealth-Other category. Finally, all the Wealth subcategories are combined into a category indicating the overall concern with economic matters, Wealth-Total. In comparison (Table 2.3), the Harvard IV dictionary scheme provides only two similar categories, Economic and Exchange.

Another perspective on classification schemes is gained by examining the assignment of words to categories. Table 2.3 presents a portion of the alphabetic list of nouns assigned to Wealth-Other. The LVD was originally constructed primarily for the analysis of political documents, such as newspaper editorials and party platforms. Thus the Wealth-Other category includes many nouns that refer to commodities, such as "corn," "tin," and so forth, because in political documents references to these commodities occur in an economic context (e.g., "The price of corn declined for the seventh consecutive month").

The numbers at the end of some words indicate the particular sense number of a word with more than one meaning (homograph). They are

**TABLE 2.1**
**Selected Lasswell Value Dictionary Categories**

| Tag | Full Name and Definition |
|-----|--------------------------|
| ENLSCOP | ENLIGHTENMENT-SCOPE-INDICATOR: Words indicating concern with wisdom, knowledge, etc. as a fundamental goal rather than a means to other ends. |
| ENLTOT | ENLIGHTENMENT-TOTAL: Indicates concern with knowledge, insight, and information concerning cultural and personal relations. Includes all entries denoting and describing academic matters and the processes which generate and communicate information, thought, and understanding. |
| NTYPE | N-TYPE WORDS: Relatively high frequency words that often lack semantic meaning, such as "a," "the," "to," forms of the verb "to be." |
| SCOPIND | SCOPE-INDICATOR: Indicates concern with ultimate end rather than with means. |
| SELVES | SELVES: First person plural pronouns. |
| SKLTOT | SKILL-TOTAL: SKILL is defined as proficiency in any practice whatever, whether in arts or crafts, trade or profession. Indicates a concern with the mastery of the physical environment and the skills and tools used to that purpose. |
| SURE | SURE: Sentiment category containing words that indicate certainty, sureness, and firmness. |
| TIMESP | TIME-SPACE: General time and space category. Contains directions, such as up, down, etc., and time indicators, such as hour, early, late. |
| UNDEF | UNDEFINED: Includes words with value implications that vary from context to context, and which, notwithstanding disambiguation routes, cannot be assessed reliably by present procedures. |
| UNDEF* | UNDEFINABLE: Includes entries that have no value implications or that have value meaning that cannot be defined in terms of the present category scheme. |
| WLTOTH | WEALTH-OTHER: Entries denoting the wealth process not classified as PARTICIPANT or TRANSACTION are classified here. |
| WLTPT | WEALTH-PARTICIPANT: Contains the generic names of the trades and professions in the wealth process. Also includes social roles related to wealth processes, such as "banker." |
| WLTTOT | WEALTH-TOTAL: Wealth is defined as income or services of goods and persons accruing to the person in any way whatsoever. All references to production resources and the accumulation or exchange of goods and services have been included in this category. |
| WLTXACT | WEALTH-TRANSACTION: Contains references to the creation or exchange of wealth, mainly verbs. |
| XACT | TRANSACTION: Residual category indicating value transactions not elsewhere classified because it could not be reliably determined whether the transaction resulted in a gain or loss or what was the object of the transaction. |

SOURCE: Adapted from Namenwirth and Weber (1984) and Lasswell and Namenwirth (1968).

**TABLE 2.2**
**Selected Harvard IV Dictionary Categories**

| Tag | Full Name and Definition |
|---|---|
| ABS* | ABSTRACT: Words indicating nontangibles or concepts. |
| AFFIL | AFFILIATION: All words with the connotation of affiliation or supportiveness. |
| CAUSAL | CAUSAL: Words denoting presumption that occurrence of one phenomenon is necessarily preceded, accompanied, or followed by the occurrence of another. |
| COLL | COLLECTIVITY: All collectivities excluding animal collectivities (ANIMAL). |
| COMFORM | COMMUNICATION FORM: All processes and forms of communication, excluding finite, concrete, visible, and tangible objects for communication (e.g., book) but does include words such as essay, fare, and chapter, where the emphasis is more on the communication transaction than on the object itself. |
| COMN | COMMUNICATION: All forms and processes of communication. |
| DOCTR | DOCTRINE: Organized system of belief or knowledge. Includes all formal bodies of knowledge (astronomy, agriculture), belief systems (Christianity, stoicism), and the arts. |
| ECON* | ECONOMIC: All words that relate to economic, commercial, and industrial matters. Includes all economic roles, collectivities, acts, abstract ideas, and symbols. Also includes references to technical industrial processes and to economic commodities such as coal and aluminum. |
| EXCH | EXCHANGE: Words indicating economic processes and transactions such as buying and selling. |
| GOAL | GOAL: Names of end-states toward which striving, muscular or mental, is directed. |
| IMPERS | IMPERSONAL: All impersonal nouns. |
| INCR | INCREASE: Words indicating increase. |
| INTREL | INTERRELATE: Interpersonal action words involving changing relationships between people, things, or ideas. Abstract nouns derived from these verbs are generally to be found in VIRTUE or VICE. |
| OUR | OUR: All pronouns that are inclusive self-references. |
| OVRST | OVERSTATE: Words providing emphasis in the following areas: speed, frequency, inevitability, causality, inclusiveness of persons, objects, or places, quantity in numerical and quasi-numerical terms, accuracy and validity, importance, intensity, likelihood, certainty, and extremity. |
| POLIT* | POLITICAL: All words with a clearly political character. Includes political roles, collectivities, acts, ideas, ideologies, and symbols. |
| POWER | POWER: All words with the connotation of power, control, or authority. |

SOURCE: Adapted from Dunphy et al. (1974).

## TABLE 2.3
## Alphabetical Listing of Wealth-Other Nouns, Lasswell
## Value Dictionary

| ***NOUNS*** | DEPRESSION#2 | IRRIGATION | RESOURCE |
|---|---|---|---|
| ABUNDANCE | DOLLAR | LEDGER | RETAIL#1 |
| ACCOUNT#2 | EARN#2 | LIABILITY#1 | RETIREMENT |
| ACRE | ECONOMICS | LIVESTOCK | RETURN#3 |
| AFFLUENCE | ECONOMIST | LOAN#1 | RICH#6 |
| AGRICULTURE | ECONOMY | LOT#3 | ROAD#1 |
| ALLOWANCE | ELECTRICITY | LOW-COST | ROYALTY#2 |
| ANNUITY | EMPLOYMENT | LUXURY | RUBBER |
| APPROPRIATION | END#6 | MANUFACTURE#1 | SALARY |
| ARTICLE#2 | ENDOWMENT | MANUFACTURER | SALESMANSHIP |
| AUTO | ENERGY | MARKET#1 | SAVE#3 |
| AUTOMOBILE | ENGINE | MARKET#2 | SCARCITY |
| BACKWARDNESS | ENTERPRISE | MERCHANDISE | SECURITY#2 |
| BALE | EQUITY | MINE#2 | SECURITY#3 |
| BANKRUPTCY | ESTATE | MINERAL | SELL#2 |
| BARGAIN#1 | EXPENDITURE | MINT | SHIFT#2 |
| BELONG#2 | EXPENSE#1 | MONEY | SHOP#1 |
| BENEFIT#1 | EXPORT#1 | MORTGAGE#1 | SHOP#3 |
| BILL#2 | FACTORY | OIL | SILK |
| BONUS | FARM#1 | ORE | STEEL |
| BOOKKEEPING | FARM#3 | OUTPUT#1 | STERLING |
| BOUNTY | FERTILIZER | OWNERSHIP | STOCK |
| BRANCH#2 | FINANCE#1 | PARITY | STORE#1 |
| BRASS | FOREST | PAY#2 | STORE#3 |
| BREAD | FORESTRY | PAYROLL | SUPPLIER |
| BUDGET | FORTUNE#2 | PENNY | SUPPLY#1 |
| BUSINESS#1 | FREIGHT | PENSION | SURPLUS |
| BUY#2 | FRUGALITY | PIECE#2 | TARIFF |
| CAPITAL | FUND#1 | PLANT#2 | TAX#1 |
| CAR | FUND#2 | PLANTATION | TAX#3 |
| CARTEL | FUR | POOR#5 | TAX#4 |
| CASH#1 | GARDEN#1 | POPULATION | TAXATION |
| CATTLE | GARDEN#2 | PORT | TEXTILE |
| CENT | GIFT | POULTRY | TIMBER |
| CHARGE#4 | GOLD | POUND#1 | TIN |
| CHECK#1 | GOODS | POVERTY | TRAIN#1 |
| CHEQUE | GRAIN | PRESENT#5 | TRANSPORT#1 |
| CLEAR#10 | GRANT#1 | PRICE | TRANSPORTATION |
| COAL | HERD#1 | PROCEED#3 | TREASURE#1 |
| COFFEE | HIDE#3 | PRODUCE#2 | TREASURER |
| COIN | HIGHWAY | PRODUCER | TREASURY |
| COLLATERAL | HOLD#4 | PRODUCTIVITY | TRUST#5 |
| COMMERCE | HORTICULTURE | PROPERTY | UNEMPLOYMENT |
| COMMODITY | HOUSEHOLD | PROSPERITY | WAGE#1 |
| COPPER | INCENTIVE | RANCH | WEALTH#1 |
| COPYRIGHT | INCOME#1 | RANCHER | WHEAT |
| CORN | INDEMNITY | RATE#1 | WHOLESALE |
| COTTON | INDUSTRIALISM | REAL#3 | WIN#3 |
| CROP#1 | INDUSTRY | RECEIPT | WOOD#1 |
| CURRENCY | INFLATION | RECLAMATION | WOOD#2 |
| CUSTOM#2 | INPUT | REDEVELOPMENT | WOOL |
| DEBT | INTEREST#2 | REFUND#1 | WORTH#3 |
| DEFICIT | INVENTORY | REMUNERATION | |
| DEPARTMENT#2 | INVESTMENT | RENT#1 | |
| DEPRECIATION | IRON#1 | RENTAL | |

SOURCE: Laswell and Namenwirth (1968).

not immediately useful without a corresponding list of the various senses of each homograph, but space limitations preclude an extensive discussion here (the interested reader is referred to Kelly and Stone, 1975).

Although categories pertaining to economic matters generally have high internal consistency in the sense that all the words have similar connotations, this is not necessarily the case with other categories. For example, the LVD lumps together words related to temporal and spatial relations. The justification for this has always been vague, and perhaps there should be a separate category for each. Similarly, the Harvard dictionary classifies words that refer to political ideologies and to political actors in the same category. Again, the justification of this strategy is unclear.

Even if the ambiguity of category definitions and word classifications can be overcome, other sources of error remain. As noted, one of the most serious problems in early computer programs for content analysis was that they could not deal with words that had more than one meaning—homographs. For example, does "kind" refer to a class of objects or a benevolent disposition? For English language text, these problems were resolved by the latest version of the General Inquirer system (Kelly and Stone, 1975). These computer programs and their associated dictionaries, the Harvard IV and the LVD, incorporate rules that distinguish among the various senses of homographs according to the context of usage. Technically known as *disambiguation rules,* these procedures lead to an important increase in the precision of text classification. With respect to content classification, higher precision refers to high accuracy when more or finer distinctions are being made. These distinctions are often semantic,[19] such as those among the various senses of homographs.

Another problem in text analysis arises from phrases or idioms that constitute a unit of meaning. Some of these phrases function as proper nouns, for example, "Sage Publications," "United Nations," or "United States of America." Others are idioms or phrases, such as "bleeding-heart liberals," "point of no return," or "a turn for the worst." Although the earliest forms of the General Inquirer included the capability to handle idioms, the latest version uses the same flexible features for handling homographs to handle idioms. Thus the investigator can choose between the individual word, word sense (of homographs), or phrase as the appropriate semantic unit.[20]

Although existing computer systems handle the ambiguity of homographs, there are other unresolved difficulties in this type of text classification. Because this software only operates on one sentence at a time, it cannot determine the referents of pronouns and ambiguous phrases, such as "this family" in the last sentence of the first example at the beginning of this chapter. Two resolutions of the problem have been employed. The first is to ignore it, with the consequence that some category counts are slight underestimations. The second strategy is to edit the text so that the referent is placed immediately after the pronoun or phrases. This method is labor-intensive, but leads to more accurate counts.[21] Here is an excerpt from the 1886 address of the British monarch before Parliament (similar to our State of the Union address) discussing Home Rule for Ireland with the referent of *it* identified by the investigator (Weber, 1982: 398):

> I have seen with deep sorrow the renewal, since I last addressed you, of the attempt to excite the people of Ireland to hostility against the legislative union between that country and Great Britain. I am resolutely opposed to any disturbance of the fundamental law, and in resisting it [any disturbance of the fundamental law] I am convinced that I shall be heartily supported by my Parliament and my people.

Table 2.4 presents a few sentences from the 1980 party platforms. Each word is followed by a list of assigned LVD categories.[22] As in the previous table, the numbers next to some words indicate the particular sense of homograph. A significant portion of the text is comprised of words that are important for the construction of sentences, but that are not assigned to a substantive LVD category. These N-type words include articles (e.g., a, the) and some prepositions (e.g., in, of). Indices are usually constructed after subtracting the number of N-type words from the total number of words. For example, dividing the number of words in a document classified in a particular category by the total minus N-type number of words in the document yields a measure interpreted as the proportion of words with relevant semantic information classified in that category.

Additional problems arise because some words may be classified in two categories, in which one is a total and the other is a subcategory. "Economy," for example, is classified as Wealth-Other and Wealth-Total. As noted, in order to maintain the statistical independence of the content variables, statistical analyses should use either the total category or one or more subcategories, but not both total and subcategories.

A major advantage of computer-aided content analysis is that the same text can be analyzed easily using more than one category scheme. In addition, the text can be reclassified after making modifications to an existing dictionary because of errors or because changes seem justified in light of the particular text being analyzed. Table 2.5 presents the same text classified according to the categories of the Harvard IV dictionary. Again, the output consists of words with the sense numbers of homographs and a list of assigned Harvard IV categories.[23]

**TABLE 2.4**
**Sample Text with LVD Tags**

| Word | Categories |
|------|-----------|

SENTENCE 7 ** DOCUMENT 1 ** IDENTIFICATION AD1980

| | |
|------|-----------|
| THE | N-TYPE |
| EFFECT#1 | SCOPE-INDICATOR |
| ON | N-TYPE |
| OUR | SELVES |
| ECONOMY | WEALTH-OTHER WEALTH-TOTAL |
| MUST#1 | UNDEFINED |
| BE#1 | N-TYPE |
| ONE#2 | UNDEFINABLE |
| WHICH | N-TYPE |
| ENCOURAGE#1S | POWER-INDULGENCE POWER-TOTAL |
| JOB | SKILL-OTHER SKILL-TOTAL |
| FORMATION | UNDEFINED |
| AND | N-TYPE |
| BUSINESS#1 | WEALTH-OTHER WEALTH-TOTAL |
| GROWTH. | SCOPE-INDICATOR |

*** START NEW DOCUMENT..
SENTENCE 8 ** DOCUMENT 2 ** IDENTIFICATION AR1980

| | |
|------|-----------|
| TAX#1ES. | WEALTH-OTHER WEALTH-TOTAL |

SENTENCE 9 ** DOCUMENT 2 ** IDENTIFICATION AR1980

| | |
|------|-----------|
| ELSEWHERE | TIME-SPACE |
| IN | N-TYPE |
| THIS#1 | N-TYPE |
| PLATFORM#1 | POWER-OTHER POWER-TOTAL |
| WE | SELVES |
| DISCUSS | ENLIGHTENMENT-SCOPE-INDICATOR ENLIGHTENMENT-TOTAL |
| THE | N-TYPE |
| BENEFIT#3S, | BASE-INDICATOR |
| FOR | N-TYPE |
| SOCIETY | COLLECTIVE-PARTICIPANT |
| AS#1 | N-TYPE |
| A | N-TYPE |
| WHOLE#2, | UNDEFINED |
| OF | N-TYPE |
| REDUCED | TRANSACTION |
| TAXATION, | WEALTH-OTHER WEALTH-TOTAL |
| PARTICULAR#4LY | SURE |
| IN | N-TYPE |
| TERM#1S | ENLIGHTENMENT-OTHER ENLIGHTENMENT-TOTAL |
| OF | N-TYPE |
| ECONOMIC | WEALTH-OTHER WEALTH-TOTAL |
| GROWTH. | SCOPE-INDICATOR |

**TABLE 2.5**
**Sample Text with HARVARD IV Tags**

| Word | Categories |
|------|------------|

SENTENCE 7 ** DOCUMENT 1 ** IDENTIFICATION AD1980

| Word | Categories |
|------|------------|
| THE | ART |
| EFFECT#1 | ABS* CAUSAL PSV |
| ON | SPACE |
| OUR | AFFIL OUR |
| ECONOMY | DOCTR ECON* |
| MUST#1 | OUGHT |
| BE#1 | BE |
| ONE#2 | INDEF OTHER |
| WHICH | INDEF INT RLTVI |
| ENCOURAGE#1S | INTREL AFFIL PSTV ACTV |
| JOB | MEANS ECON* |
| FORMATION | MEANS STRNG |
| AND | CONJ1 |
| BUSINESS#1 | DOCTR ECON* |
| GROWTH. | STRNG INCR PSV |

*** START NEW DOCUMENT..
SENTENCE 8 ** DOCUMENT 2 ** IDENTIFICATION AR1980

| Word | Categories |
|------|------------|
| TAX#1ES. | MEANS POLIT ECON* |

SENTENCE 9 ** DOCUMENT 2 ** IDENTIFICATION AR1980

| Word | Categories |
|------|------------|
| ELSEWHERE | SPACE |
| IN | SPACE |
| THIS#1 | DEM DEM1 |
| PLATFORM#1 | DOCTR POLIT* |
| WE | PLRLP OUR |
| DISCUSS | PSTV COMFORM |
| THE | ART |
| BENEFIT#3S, | GOAL PSTV STRNG |
| FOR | CONJ CONJ2 |
| SOCIETY | COLL POLIT* |
| AS#1 | CONJ2 CAUSAL |
| A | ART |
| WHOLE#2, | QUAN STRNG OVRST |
| OF | PREP |
| REDUCED | DECR STRNG |
| TAXATION, | MEANS POLIT ECON* |
| PARTICULAR#4LY | OVRST |
| IN | SPACE |
| TERM#1S | COM COMFORM |
| OF | PREP |
| ECONOMIC | POLIT DOCTR ECON* |
| GROWTH. | STRNG INCR PSV |

Several ways of manipulating, classifying, and analyzing text are presented in Chapter 3. The remainder of this chapter discusses several important problems in the construction of category schemes and text classification.

## Single Versus Multiple Classification

In classifying a word or other recording unit into a particular dictionary category, one really answers the question: Does the entry generally have a certain attribute (or set of interrelated attributes)? Two answers to this question exist: Yes, the entry does, and it is therefore thus classified. Or, the answer is no, and therefore the entry is not classified under this heading. This formulation points at two complications. First, having one attribute does not logically exclude the possession of another. Second, not all entries need have the same attribute to the same extent. The qualities by which words are classified may be continuous rather than dichotomous, thus leading to variation in intensity.[24] Double or multiple classification of entries resolves the first problem, but creates others.

Different strategies have been followed to resolve these issues. For example, the design of the Lasswell dictionary assumes that the gain in semantic precision does not outweigh the loss of logical distinctiveness and exclusiveness (Namenwirth and Weber, 1984; Lasswell and Namenwirth, 1968). Logical exclusiveness is a precarious precondition of all classification for subsequent statistical analysis. Therefore, in the Lasswell dictionary, if an entry can be classified under more than one category it is classified in the category that seems most appropriate, most of the time, for most texts. As for intensity, although it is true that not all category entries will have the same pertinence to the category, a dichotomous rather than weighted classification scheme is employed nonetheless.

The category scheme of the current Harvard dictionary was constructed using a very different strategy (Dunphy et al., 1974). It has a set of "first-order" categories in which entries can be assigned on a hierarchical basis if warranted. These first-order categories represent the basic analytic categories. Figure 2.1 illustrates the hierarchical nature of the Harvard first-order categories that deal with psychological states. Two categories, Need and Perceive, have no subcategories, but Feel, Think, and Evaluation do.

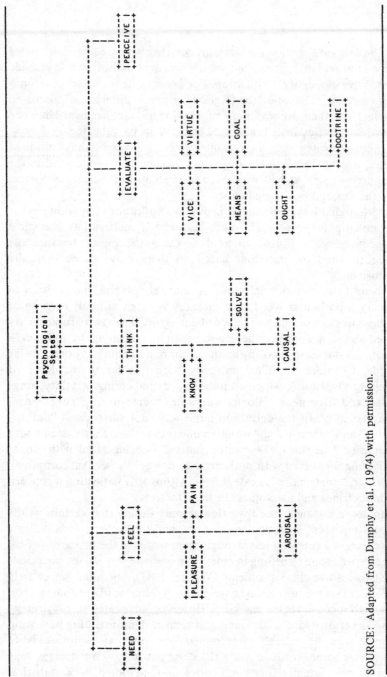

SOURCE: Adapted from Dunphy et al. (1974) with permission.

Figure 2.1: Harvard IV Dictionary First-Order Categories, "Psychological States"

The Harvard dictionary contains another set of categories, called "second order" categories, that are independent of the first and provide alternative modes of classification. For example, there is a set of second-order categories based on the Osgood "semantic differential" discussed above. How, then, are words classified using this architecture? The word "abstract" is classified both in Think and in its subcategory Know. "Absence" is categorized in the same two categories with the addition of Weak, one of the Osgood categories. "Acceptable" is classified in the first order Think and Evaluation, the Evaluation subcategory Virtue, and the Osgood Positive category.

Although this type of scheme provides a multitude of possibilities for the investigator, great care must be taken if multivariate statistical procedures will be used to analyze category counts, because the categories and the variables based on them may not be mutually exclusive.

Even if the category definition is relatively precise, the decision to classify a particular word in a category is often difficult because of ambiguities in word meaning. Word ambiguity poses two problems. As noted above, a word may have more than one meaning. In addition, a word may not seem as strong an indicator of a category as other similar words. Consider the LVD category Sure (similar to the Harvard category Overstate), which contains words indicating certainty, sureness, and firmness. Words such as "certainly," "sure," and "emphatically" fit the definition quite well. But what about "authoritative" and "doctrinaire," which in one thesaurus are also listed under "certainty"? In the LVD, "authoritative" is categorized with words indicating a concern with authoritative power (Power-Authoritative); however, "doctrinaire" is categorized with words indicating a concern with doctrines and ideologies (Power-Doctrine).

In some instances the investigator may decide that certain words clearly represent a particular category, and that other words indicate or represent a category less strongly than words in the first group. Still other words seem to belong in more than one category. Many proposals exist to resolve these problems (Weber, 1983), but none are entirely satisfactory. One solution is to weight each other word depending upon how well it connotes the category. However, advocates of this strategy have never provided a convincing argument demonstrating how valid weights can be reliably determined. An alternate solution is to categorize some words in more than one category. This strategy may lead to conceptually fuzzy categories that, as noted, lack statistical independence.

Perhaps the best practical strategy is to classify each word, word sense, or phrase in the category in which it most clearly belongs. If there is sufficient ambiguity, the word should be dropped from the category and if necessary, from analysis. This tactic restricts categories to those words that unmistakably indicate concern with the category, thereby maximizing validity. However, some words of substantive interest may not be analyzed because they are not clear indicators of a particular category. Each investigator will have to find the resolution that makes the most sense in light of the goals of the analysis.

## Assumed Versus Inferred Categories

Compared with hand-coding, computer-based content analysis has the advantage that one set of texts can be easily classified by more than one dictionary. However, this generates multiple descriptions of the same textual reality. Consequently, an important debate exists over whose classification scheme should be used. Some (Stone et al., 1966; Dunphy et al., 1974; Namenwirth and Weber, 1974) hold that the category scheme should be theoretically justified, and that therefore the investigator's categories should be used. For example, the earliest Harvard Psychosocial dictionaries were based in part on Parsonian and Freudian concepts (Stone et al., 1966); the Lasswell Value Dictionary (Lasswell and Namenwirth, 1968; Namenwirth and Weber, 1984) is predicated on Lasswell and Kaplan's (1950) conceptual scheme for political analysis.[25]

Others (e.g., Iker and Harway, 1969; Cleveland et al., 1974; Krippendorff, 1980: 126) argue that assumed category schemes impose the reality of the investigator on the text. The better course of action uses the categories of those who produced the text.[26] These categories are frequently inferred from covariation among high-frequency words using factor analysis or similar techniques.[27]

This dispute stems both from difficult methodological problems and from conceptual confusion. Specifically, let the term "category" be reserved for groups of words with *similar* meanings or connotations (Stone et al., 1966; Dunphy et al., 1974). The words "banker," "money," and "mortgage" might be classified in a Wealth or Economic category. Now let the term "theme" refer to clusters of words with *different* meanings or connotations that taken together refer to some theme or issue. For instance, the sentence, "New York bankers invest money in many industries both at home and abroad" in part reflects concern with an Economic theme. The disagreement over categories is largely a dispute between those who define categories as words with different meanings or connotations that covary empirically (inferred categories), and those who define categories as words with similar meanings or connotations that do not covary (assumed categories). Words classified as Economic, for example, will tend to covary with words in other categories, say Power, Uncertainty, or Well-Being, rather than with other Economic words.

Terminology aside, in studies based on inferred categories, different category schemes arise from different sets of texts. Advocates of inferred categories have failed to recognize that this multitude of categories requires a theory of categories. Such a theory would explain the range of possible categories and the empirically observed variation in category schemes (Namenwirth and Weber, 1974). Without such a theory, research based on inferred categories is unlikely to lead to the cumulation of comparable results.

## Alternative Classification Schemes
## and Substantive Results

The choice of classification schemes is in part predicated on theoretical considerations. For example, if one wishes to study extensively a particular construct, such as McClelland's Need Achievement (Nach), then one might construct a dictionary that scores only that variable (e.g., Stone et al., 1966: 191ff). General dictionaries follow a different strategy based on many "common sense" categories of meaning. These categories are chosen to reflect the wide range of human experience and understanding encoded in language.

Having decided to employ the strategy of general dictionaries, the choice of one rather than another content classification scheme has little or no effect on the substantive results. That is, if the same text is classified using different general dictionaries (and analogous measurement models, see Weber, 1983), then one will arrive at the same substantive conclusions.

Empirical evidence supports this point (Namenwirth and Bibbee, 1975: 61). In their analysis of newspaper editorials, Namenwirth and Bibbee classified the text using two different dictionaries and then factor analyzed the two sets of scores separately. Comparing the results across dictionaries, Namenwirth and Bibbee found that the factors had similar interpretations. Furthermore, irrespective of which dictionary was used, Namenwirth and Bibbee arrived at similar substantive conclusions.[28]

This evidence is suggestive rather than conclusive. Consequently, future research should investigate the relationship between the dictionary used to classify text and the substantive conclusions. Texts can be classified with more than one dictionary and the results compared. If the substantive conclusions do not depend on the particular category scheme, researchers reluctant to use one or another existing dictionary that does not operationalize their particular conceptual scheme might then be persuaded to do so. In addition, those who might create dictionaries in languages other than English might be persuaded to utilize existing category schemes to maintain cross-language comparability of results.

In the event that the results only partially replicate across dictionaries, additional research should ascertain the circumstances under which the results are similar and variant.

## Units of Aggregation Problems

After assigning the words in the text to various categories, the investigator usually aggregates these counts into numbers that represent the intensity of concern with each category in the document.[29] However, the choice of document as the logical aggregate unit of analysis is only one of several possibilities. For example, one might use sentences, paragraphs, or themes. There is some evidence (Saris-Gallhofer et al., 1978; Grey et al., 1965) indicating that the reliability of content categories varies by the level of aggregation: In a comparison of hand- and computer-coded content analysis of the same texts, sentences and documents had the highest reliabilities, while the reliability for paragraphs was slightly lower. In addition, the reliability at all levels of aggregation was substantially less than the reliabilities for specific words or phrases.

Using people to code *New York Times* editorials that appeared during World War II, Grey et al. (1965) found that the substantive conclusions were affected by the type of recording unit. They coded a sample of editorials using four different units of text:

- symbols that correspond to words or short phrases;
- paragraphs;
- units of three sentences; and
- whole editorials.

They also coded each unit of text as being favorable, neutral, or unfavorable toward the symbol. Controlling for the total number of each type, they found that longer coding units (paragraphs, whole editorials) produced a greater proportion of units scored favorable or unfavorable and fewer units scored neutral than did the shorter units.

These findings call into question long-standing practices regarding aggregation of words into larger units in both hand-coded and computer-aided content analysis. Future research should investigate the relationships among substantive conclusions, reliability, validity, and different levels of aggregation.

## Concluding Remarks

Some problems of content analysis are well known. Others require further investigation using modern statistical techniques and methodological insights (Weber, 1983). The article by Saris-Gallhofer and her associates (1978) mentioned above is a model of the kind of research that is required if content analysis is to be put on a more solid footing. Even though much basic research remains to be done, the accumulated results of the last 15 years suggest that for many kinds of problems, existing techniques of content analysis lead to valid and theoretically interesting results. Many of these techniques are discussed in the next chapter.

## Suggestions for Further Reading

The symposium papers edited by Gerbner et al. (1969) address many methodological issues and are still valuable reading. Kelly and Stone (1975) discuss problems in distinguishing among the various senses of words with multiple meanings. They developed one solution to this problem using procedures that are sensitive to the semantic context in which each word appears. Other approaches to understanding natural language text are cited at the end of Chapter 4 in this volume.

Validity and reliability in their most general sense are discussed in Campbell and Stanley (1963), Cook and Campbell (1979), Brinberg and Kidder (1982), Carmines and Zeller (1982), Zeller and Carmines (1980), Lord and Novick (1968), and some of the works in Blalock (1974), to cite several possibilities. The *Sociological Methodology* series published by Jossey-Bass and sponsored by the ASA includes many articles on validity and reliability assessment.

## 3. TECHNIQUES OF CONTENT ANALYSIS

One of the most important advantages of computer-aided content analysis over hand-coded or interpretive content analysis is that the rules for coding text are made explicit. The public nature of the coding rules yields tools for inquiry that, when applied to a variety of texts, generate formally comparable results. Over time, this comparability should lead to the cumulation of research findings.

A second major advantage of computer-aided content analysis is that, once formalized in terms of computer programs and/or content-coding schemes, the computer provides perfect coder reliability in the application of coding rules to text. High coder reliability then frees the investigator to concentrate on other aspects of inquiry such as validity, interpretation, and explanation.

However, even with the assistance of computers, one major difficulty of content analysis is that there is too much information in texts. Their richness and detail preclude analysis without some form of data reduction. The key to content analysis, and indeed to all modes of inquiry, is choosing a strategy for information loss that yields substantively interesting and theoretically useful generalizations while reducing the amount of information addressed by the analyst.

This chapter presents a wide variety of techniques for content analysis that researchers can draw upon in future research. The investigator can tailor the methodology to the requirements of her or his particular study by selecting particular techniques. The central focus here is on computer-based content analysis as a means of text manipulation, data reduction, and data analysis in which the word or phrase is the basic unit. Several ways of manipulating text are illustrated, including word frequency counts, key-word-in-context (KWIC) listing, concordances, classification of words into content categories, content category counts, and retrievals based on content categories and co-occurrences.

The most important uses of content analysis are in research designs that relate content to noncontent variables. Other, more advanced approaches to content analysis use exploratory and confirmatory factor analysis to identify themes in texts. Analysis of variance and structural equation models are often used to relate these themes to other variables. For instance, this chapter discusses research indicating that the content of newspaper editorials varies according to the type of newspaper (mass market or elite). Another example shows how the content of the speeches of the German kaiser responded to changing economic conditions. These advanced examples are discussed in some detail in order to clarify the logic of inquiry they entail and to clarify the substantive issues addressed. Although this chapter presents examples drawn mainly from political sociology and political science, the techniques shown here can be applied to documents from many sources.

## Document Selection and Sampling

Although some studies make use of an entire population of documents, most do not. Sampling is employed primarily for the sake of economy. For content analysis, three sampling populations exist:

- communication sources;
- documents; and
- text within documents.

The sampling scheme employed will depend in large part upon the population to be sampled and the kind of inferences to be made. Among the communication sources that might be sampled are newspapers, magazines, and authors. To draw a sample, the universe must first be identified. For instance, the universe of newspapers published in America is listed in the *Ayer Directory of Publications*.

If an investigator were interested in editorial opinions in American newspapers, she or he could take a simple random sample[30] that would be representative of the population of newspapers. However, suppose empirical evidence or theory suggested that editorial opinions varied by region of the country and by frequency of publication (weekly versus daily). To ensure that the sample includes an adequate number of weekly and daily papers in each region of the country, the sampling design might call for stratified sampling.[31] In this case, the population of newspapers would first be divided by region and frequency of publication. Each of the resulting subpopulations would then be sampled randomly. This type of sampling design ensures that the final sample contains adequate numbers of newspapers from each subpopulation, and, more importantly, that the final sample is representative of the universe of daily and weekly newspapers in each region.

After identifying the communication sources to be studied, the investigator may reduce the amount of text to be analyzed by sampling documents. Researchers must be careful, however, not to introduce bias into the study by failing to take into account the conditions under which the documents are produced. For instance, consider a sample of editorials from two newspapers published both weekdays and Sunday. Suppose that the sample is to be representative of editorials in both papers over a two-year period. Also suppose that the purpose of the study is to compare and contrast editorial concerns. Several factors will have to be taken into account. First, newspapers usually publish several editorials per day and generally order them by importance on the editorial page. Second, editorials may vary by day of the week, with the less serious ones coming on weekends rather than on weekdays. In addition, editorial writers often take note of major holidays and the arrival and departure of the seasons. The sampling design must control for these systematic sources of variation in editorial content. For example, one might want to analyze only the first editorial that appears in each newspaper each nonholiday of a randomly selected week within each of the 24 months covered by the study.

Editorials are short documents. For longer texts, such as speeches or books, economy may suggest that sampling be employed. Here again the investigator must take into account the nature of the texts. For example, speeches such as presidential acceptance speeches, State of the Union addresses, and the British Queen's Speech from the Throne tend to have a form or organization that reflects the partly ritualized nature of these texts. There are often routine introductions and closings. Domestic and financial affairs may be addressed before foreign affairs.

When possible, the entire text should be analyzed. This preserves the semantic coherence of texts as units. However, if sampling is required, then the investigator must take into account the structure of the text. For instance, the introductory and closing sections might be excluded. Portions dealing with domestic and foreign matters might be sampled separately. If the researcher must sample text within documents, each sample should consist of one or more whole paragraphs. This preserves some degree of semantic coherence. Sentences should *not* be sampled, because analyzing sentences in isolation—even ones drawn from the same text—destroys semantic coherence, making validation and interpretation extremely difficult.

## Text Encoding

After selecting the documents to be analyzed, the investigator must convert the text to a format and on a medium readable by the computer (i.e., machine-readable). In the early days of computers this process was notoriously costly and error-prone. The text was encoded by punching different patterns of holes in cards to represent different letters, numbers, and special characters (e.g., dollar signs and ampersands). Often the same text was punched twice in order to locate errors, a process called *verification*. It was not unusual for text entry to take up a large part of a modest research budget. For example, one project took about 9 person-months to keypunch, proofread, and correct almost a half million words and punctuation.

Today, researchers can employ an optical scanner that reads almost any typed or printed page and then transfers the text to an electronic storage medium such as tape or disk. This device, the Kurzweil Data Entry Machine[32] (KDEM), is very accurate and fast. Businesses across the country[33] serving the general public use the KDEM to scan printed material. These firms will scan newspapers, magazines, typescripts, and so on at nominal cost—often for one or two dollars per thousand characters or less, depending upon the quality of the printing. At present, however, no optical scanning facility exists for handwritten text.

To assess the latest model of the KDEM, a test was performed using the 1980 Democratic and Republican party platforms (Johnson, 1982). These documents consist of approximately 470,000 characters or 100,000 words and punctuation. The KDEM took 4.5 hours to scan these documents, yielding an overall rate of about 30 characters per second. A minimum amount of editing was done during the entry process to check characters that were questioned by the KDEM.[34] The final output had fewer than 50 characters in error, representing an accuracy rate of 99.9%.

## Key-Word-In-Context
## Lists and Concordances

One of the first things the investigator wants to know is which words appear in the text and how they are actually used. KWIC (Key-Word-In-Context) lists (Table 3.1) show the context in which each word appears. This information can be used in a variety of ways. First, KWIC lists draw attention to the variation or consistency in word meaning and

## TABLE 3.1

## Selected Key-Word-In-Context Records for Word "Rights," 1980 Republican and Democrat Party Platforms

### 1980 Reagan Republican Platform

| | | | |
|---|---|---|---|
| YOUNG PEOPLE WANT THE OPPORTUNITY TO EXERCISE THE | RIGHTS | AND RESPONSIBILITIES OF ADULTS. THE REPUBLICAN PA | AR1980 | 372 |
| ACTERIZED BY THE HIGHEST REGARD FOR PROTECTING THE | RIGHTS | OF LAW-ABIDING CITIZENS, AND IS CONSISTENT WITH T | AR1980 | 1004 |
| OF THEIR SCHOOL SYSTEMS. WE WILL RESPECT THE | RIGHTS | OF STATE AND LOCAL AUTHORITIES IN THE MANAGEMENT | AR1980 | 333 |
| RIGHTS AND THE HELSINKI AGREEMENTS WHICH GUARANTEE | RIGHTS | SUCH AS THE FREE INTERCHANGE OF INFORMATION AND T | AR1980 | 1391 |
| UALLY AND STEADFASTLY COMMITTED TO THE EQUALITY OF | RIGHTS | FOR ALL CITIZENS, REGARDLESS OF RACE. AS THE PART | AR1980 | 206 |
| S ISSUES, IS ULTIMATELY CONCERNED WITH EQUALITY OF | RIGHTS | UNDER THE LAW. THERE CAN BE NO DOUBT THAT THE QUE | AR1980 | 284 |
| SE WHO SUPPORT OR OPPOSE RATIFICATION OF THE EQUAL | RIGHTS | AMENDMENT. WE ACKNOWLEDGE THE LEGITIMATE EFFORTS | AR1980 | 227 |
| SSION ARE IN THE COURTS. RATIFICATION OF THE EQUAL | RIGHTS | AMENDMENT IS NOW IN THE HANDS OF STATE LEGISLATUR | AR1980 | 232 |
| REAFFIRM OUR PARTY'S HISTORIC COMMITMENT TO EQUAL | RIGHTS | AND EQUALITY FOR WOMEN. | AR1980 | 228 |
| XEMPTION FROM THE MILITARY DRAFT. WE SUPPORT EQUAL | RIGHTS | AND EQUAL OPPORTUNITIES FOR WOMEN, WITHOUT TAKING | AR1980 | 229 |
| ON POLICY MUST BE BASED ON THE PRIMACY OF PARENTAL | RIGHTS | AND RESPONSIBILITY. FEDERAL EDUCATI | AR1980 | 322 |
| N'S COMMITMENT TO DEFEND THEM, INDIVIDUAL | RIGHTS | AND SOCIETAL VALUES ARE ONLY AS STRONG AS A NATIO | AR1980 | 152 |
| MULTIRACIAL SOCIETY WITH GUARANTEES OF INDIVIDUAL | RIGHTS | IS POSSIBLE AND CAN WORK. REPUBLICANS BELIEVE THA | AR1980 | 1557 |
| VE ECONOMIC SECURITY. HISPANICS SEEK ONLY THE FULL | RIGHTS | OF CITIZENSHIP -- IN EDUCATION, IN LAW ENFORCEMEN | AR1980 | 213 |
| UNITIES FOR WOMEN, WITHOUT TAKING AWAY TRADITIONAL | RIGHTS | OF WOMEN SUCH AS EXEMPTION FROM THE MILITARY DRAF | AR1980 | 229 |
| ING STRONG, EFFECTIVE ENFORCEMENT OF FEDERAL CIVIL | RIGHTS | STATUTES, ESPECIALLY THOSE DE DURING THE NEXT FOU | AR1980 | 209 |
| CARE IS DEREGULATION AND AN EMPHASIS UPON CONSUMER | RIGHTS | AND PATIENT CHOICE. THE PRESCRIPTION FOR GOOD HEA | AR1980 | 350 |
| IMPLEMENT THE UNITED NATIONS DECLARATION ON HUMAN | RIGHTS | AND THE HELSINKI AGREEMENTS WHICH GUARANTEE RIGHT | AR1980 | 1391 |
| THEIR EMIGRATION IS A FUNDAMENTAL AFFRONT TO HUMAN | RIGHTS | AND THE U.N THE DECLINE IN EXIT VISAS TO SOVIET J | AR1980 | 1394 |
| BEEN DURING THE CARTER ADMINISTRATION. HUMAN | RIGHTS | IN THE SOVIET UNION WILL NOT BE IGNORED AS IT HAS | AR1980 | 1398 |
| N'S RHETORIC, THE MOST FLAGRANT OFFENDERS OF HUMAN | RIGHTS | INCLUDING THE SOVIET UNION, VIETNAM, AND CUBA HAV | AR1980 | 1072 |
| NS LINKED TO ITS UNDIFFERENTIATED CHARGES OF HUMAN | RIGHTS | VIOLATIONS. YET, THE CARTER ADMINISTRATION'S POLI | AR1980 | 1473 |

(continued)

# TABLE 3.1 Continued

## 1980 Carter Democratic Platform

| Left context | | Right context | Source | No. |
|---|---|---|---|---|
| FAIR SHARE OF OUR ECONOMY. WE PLEDGE TO SECURE THE | RIGHTS | OF WORKING WOMEN, HOMEMAKERS, MINORITY WOMEN AND | AD1980 | 255 |
| CH ARE IN OUR CURRENT LAWS IN ORDER TO VIOLATE THE | RIGHTS | OF THOSE ATTEMPTING TO ORGANIZE. WE CAN NO LONGER | AD1980 | 194 |
| . AS THAT EFFORT PROCEEDS, WE MUST ENSURE THAT THE | RIGHTS | OF WORKERS TO ENGAGE IN PEACEFUL PICKETING DURING | AD1980 | 1042 |
| EPENDENT CONSUMER PROTECTION AGENCY 'TO PROTECT THE | RIGHTS | AND INTERESTS OF CONSUMERS. WE PLEDGE CONTINUED S | AD1980 | 301 |
| EMPHASIZED THE INTENT OF CONGRESS ''TO PROTECT THE | RIGHTS | OF STATE AND LOCAL GOVERNMENTS AND PUBLIC AND PRI | AD1980 | 579 |
| MENT OF THE CYPRUS PROBLEM BASED ON THE LEGITIMATE | RIGHTS | OF THE TWO COMMUNITIES. WE AGREE WITH SECRETARY G | AD1980 | 1627 |
| H MANY AMERICANS HAVE ABOUT ABORTION. REPRODUCTIVE | RIGHTS | -- WE FULLY RECOGNIZE THE RELIGIOUS AND ETHICAL C | AD1980 | 374 |
| UILDING TRADES WORKERS THE SAME PEACEFUL PICKETING | RIGHTS | CURRENTLY AFFORDED INDUSTRIAL WORKERS. LEGISLATIO | AD1980 | 203 |
| ORTS. BOTH THE ERA AND DISTRICT OF COLUMBIA VOTING | RIGHTS | AMENDMENTS TO THE CONSTITUTION MUST BE RATIFIED A | AD1980 | 858 |
| ST ENFORCE VIGOROUSLY THE AMENDMENTS TO THE VOTING | RIGHTS | ACT OF 1975 TO ASSIST HISPANIC CITIZENS. TO END D | AD1980 | 861 |
| TO BARGAIN COLLECTIVELY, WHILE ENSURING THE LEGAL | RIGHTS | OF FARMERS. FARM LABOR--WE MUST VIGOROUSLY ENFORC | AD1980 | 1286 |
| TION TO RESPECT FULLY THE HUMAN AND CONSTITUTIONAL | RIGHTS | OF ALL WITHIN OUR BORDERS. THE DEMOCRATIC PARTY A | AD1980 | 846 |
| E TO THAT NEW HORIZON IS RATIFICATION OF THE EQUAL | RIGHTS | AMENDMENT. THE PRIMARY ROUT | AD1980 | 819 |
| ING, EDUCATION, WELFARE AND SOCIAL SERVICES, EQUAL | RIGHTS | AMENDMENT. | AD1980 | 809 |
| S OF GOVERNMENT WITH FULL PROTECTION FOR THE CIVIL | RIGHTS | , AND CARE FOR THE DISABLED, ELDERLY AND VETERANS, | AD1980 | 335 |
|  | RIGHTS | , AND LIBERTIES OF AMERICAN CITIZENS LIVING AT HOME | AD1980 | 873 |
| THE FAIR HOUSING ACT AND TITLE VI OF THE CIVIL | RIGHTS | ACT MUST BE AMENDED TO INCLUDE THE HANDICAPPED. | AD1980 | 901 |
| NITY PROGRAMS, TITLE VI AND TITLE VII OF THE CIVIL | RIGHTS | ACT, THE FAIR HOUSING LAWS, AND AFFIRMATIVE ACTIO | AD1980 | 834 |
| T INVESTIGATION AND PROSECUTION OF SUSPECTED CIVIL | RIGHTS | VIOLATIONS. ATTORNEYS' OFFICES, AND SWIF | AD1980 | 1060 |
| ONVENTION AND THE INTERNATIONAL COVENANTS ON HUMAN | RIGHTS | AS SOON AS POSSIBLE. WE SUPPORT SENATE RATIFICATI | AD1980 | 1529 |
| D GUARANTEE FULL PROTECTION OF THE CIVIL AND HUMAN | RIGHTS | OF ALL WORKERS. WE MUST RECOGNIZE THE VALUE OF CU | AD1980 | 862 |
| TIONS, WE WILL ACTIVELY PROMOTE THE CAUSE OF HUMAN | RIGHTS | AND EXPRESS AMERICA'S ABHORRENCE OF THE DENIAL OF | AD1980 | 1732 |
| DING SOUTH AFRICA. WE MUST BE VIGILANT ABOUT HUMAN | RIGHTS | VIOLATIONS IN ANY COUNTRY IN WHICH THEY OCCUR INC | AD1980 | 1527 |
| GROUPS, ASSERT OUR SUPPORT OF THE COURAGEOUS HUMAN | RIGHTS | ADVOCATE, NOBEL PEACE PRIZE WINNER, DR. WE SALUTE | AD1980 | 1478 |
| ETWEEN OUR TWO COUNTRIES. WE WILL PURSUE OUR HUMAN | RIGHTS | CONCERNS AS A NECESSARY PART OF OVERALL PROGRESS. | AD1980 | 1474 |
| 980 IS NOT ONLY IDENTIFIED WITH THE CAUSE OF HUMAN | RIGHTS | AND DEMOCRACY. BUT ALSO WE HAVE OPENED A NEW CHAP | AD1980 | 1748 |
| LEGISLATION DESIGNED TO GIVE PROTECTION AND HUMAN | RIGHTS | TO THOSE WORKERS AFFECTED BY PLANT CLOSINGS. WE S | AD1980 | 208 |
| ON OF UNIVERSALLY RECOGNIZED AND FUNDAMENTAL HUMAN | RIGHTS | THROUGHOUT THE AMERICAS BY URGING THAT THE SENATE | AD1980 | 1758 |
| EXCEPT FOR CLEARLY HUMANITARIAN PURPOSES TO HUMAN | RIGHTS | VIOLATORS. WE WILL UPHOLD OUR OWN LAW AND TERMINA | AD1980 | 1760 |

usage.[35] Second, KWIC lists provide systematic information that is helpful in determining whether the meaning of particular words is dependent upon their use in certain phrases or idioms. If so, the investigator will have to analyze the phrase or idiom as a single semantic unit.

Table 3.1 presents excerpts from the KWIC listing for the word "rights" in the 1980 party platforms. The two right-most columns in the table, the document identification field (e.g., *American Democrats 1980*) and the sentence number within each document, exist for cross reference. The computer program used to generate the KWIC list does not deal with word endings (suffixes); consequently, suffixes remain intact. Thus, retrieval of sentences with "rights" excludes sentences that contain only "right." Note that the KWIC list shows the larger context of word usuage,[36] and highlights syntactical and semantic differences. For instance, "rights" occurs most frequently as a noun, but there are a few occasions in which it functions as an adjective, as in "equal rights amendment."

Table 3.2 presents a KWIC list for the word "state" in which the computer has distinguished among various senses and idioms. The instructions contained in this particular dictionary permit the identification of four different senses[37] of "state":

- state (noun), such as body politic—area of government
- situation, such as "state of science"
- "to state" (verb), to declare
- "united states" (idiom)—handled by the second sense of "United"

A KWIC list can be thought of as a concordance, a listing by word of each word in the text together with its context (Preston and Coleman, 1978; Burton, 1981; 1982; Hockey and Marriot, 1982). Often used in literary or biblical studies, concordances provide a rich data base for detailed studies of word usage in all kinds of texts. For example, Brunner (1983; Brunner and Livornese, 1982; 1984) is generating a concordance of post-World War II American State of the Union addresses. From this concordance, which will be published and publicly available, investigators will be able to study how different presidents used the same word, phrase, or idiom, as in the example of "states" presented in Table 3.2.

Concordances do not automatically indicate the referents of pronouns and ambiguous phrases. Furthermore, unlike retrievals from text based on category assignments, which are discussed later in the chapter, concordances do not help to organize the text based on synonyms or words with similar connotations. However, a concordance or KWIC list with sentence identification numbers makes it easy for the investigator to examine a sentence in its larger textual context. This examination will often reveal synonyms or pronouns that need to be taken into account.

Although concordances and KWIC lists provide essential information concerning symbol usage, they are, at least initially, data expanding rather than data reducing techniques. If the concordance presents each word with three words to the left or the right, for example, obviously the original text is expanded by a factor of six. How, then, can the investigator narrow her or his focus? Concordances lend themselves to the intensive study of a few specific symbols, such as "equal rights amendment" or "women." Consequently, investigators will have to translate substantive hypotheses into concern with specific symbols.

## Word Frequency Lists

Researchers may obtain another perspective on texts by examining the highest frequency words, because each accounts for a relatively large proportion of the text. Indeed, many content analysts focus their efforts on the more frequently occurring words. Table 3.3 presents ordered word frequency lists for the 1976 and 1980 Democratic and Republican party platforms.[38] Three aspects of this table deserve mention. First, the computer program that generated these lists[39] was instructed to omit certain relatively frequent words that are usually substantively uninteresting—for example, articles such as "a" and "the," and forms of the verbs "to be," such as "is" and "was."[40] However, these words could easily have been included. The program also omitted one- and two-letter words. Second, as with the KWIC lists, the computer program used to generate word frequencies does not deal with word endings (suffixes). Consequently, "Republican" and "Republicans" appear as separate entries. Third, there are many more low-frequency than high-frequency words. In the 1980 Republican platform, for example, there are 4719 different word forms, of which 2317, or slightly less than half, occur only once (data not shown) This relatively large proportion of infrequently occurring word forms is found in all naturally occurring texts (i.e., those not constructed for special purposes, such as linguistic analysis). Analyzing the many low-frequency words is not very parsimonious, and as noted, researchers often focus their attention on the fewer high frequency words.

# TABLE 3.2
## Selected Key-Word-In-Context Records for Word "State," 1980 Republican and Democratic Party Platforms, Disambiguated Text

### 1980 Reagan Republican Platform

| Left context | Keyword | Right context | | |
|---|---|---|---|---|
| ERNMENT OF NICARAGUA . WE DO2 NOT SUPPORT1 UNITE2D | STATES | ASSISTANCE TO2 ANY1 MARXIST GOVERNMENT IN THIS1 H | AR1980 | 1423 |
| NOW , WE HAVE2 TO1 PUT1 THE UNITED | STATES | BACK1 ON THE WORLD EXPORT1 MAP . | AR1980 | 1535 |
| NUCLEAR POWER1 WOULD OVERTAKE THAT2 OF THE UNITE2D | STATES | BY THE EARLY1 1980 S , THREATENING THE SURVIVAL O | AR1980 | 1099 |
| STRENGTH . REPUBLICANS BELIEVE1 THAT1 THE UNITE2D | STATES | CAN ONLY2 NEGOTIATE WITH THE SOVIET UN ON3 FROM A | AR1980 | 1329 |
| ND EVENTUALLY A MILITARY CATASTROPHY . THE UNITE2D | STATES | CANNOT ABDICATE THAT1 ROLE WITHOUT INDUCEING A DI | AR1980 | 1113 |
| UTION TO2 THE PROBLEM OF INEQUALITY OF THE UNITE2D | STATES | CITIZENS OF PUERTO RICO WITHIN THE FRAMEWORK OF T | AR1980 | 295 |
| AT1 THE MOST1 EFFECTIVE WEAPONS AGAINST CRIME ARE1 | STATE1 | AND LOCAL AGENCYIES . ALTHOUGH WE RECOGNIZE THE V | AR1980 | 533 |
| FAMILYIES , INTOLERABLE PRESSURE1S WILL1 BUILD1 ON | STATE1 | , LOCAL , AND FEDERAL BUDGETS AS1 TAX1 REVENUES D | AR1980 | 504 |
| OF TURN3ING THE POOR5 INTO PERMANENT WARDS OF THE | STATE1 | , TRADE2ING THEIR POLITICAL SUPPORT2 FOR CONTINUE | AR1980 | 213 |
| CIAL1 WELFARE2 AGENCYIES AND STRENGTHEN1 LOCAL AND | STATE1 | ADMINISTRATIVE FUNCTION2S AND - BETTER3 COORDIN | AR1980 | 148 |
| ADMIT1TED INTO THE UNION1 AS1 A FULL4LY SOVEREIGN1 | STATE1 | AFTER1 THEY FREE3LY SO1 DETERMINE1 . THE REPUBLIC | AR1980 | 294 |
| EQUAL1 RIGHT1S AMENDMENT IS1 NOW IN THE HAND1S OF | STATE1 | LEGISLATURES , AND THE ISSUE3S OF THE TIME1 EXTEN | AR1980 | 246 |
| WLEDGE THE FUNDAMENTAL RIGHT2 TO2 EXISTENCE OF THE | STATE1 | OF ISRAEL IS1 WRONG1 . THE IMPUTATION OF LEGITIMA | AR1980 | 1397 |
| 1 . WE BELIEVE1 THE ESTABLISHMENT OF A PALESTINIAN | STATE1 | IN THE WEST BANK2 WOULD BE2 DESTABILIZING AND HAR | AR1980 | 1399 |
| E1 GOVERNMENTS WHICH WILL1 NOT DESTROY TRADITIONAL | STATE1 | SUPREMACY IN WATER1 LAW . WE MUST1 DEVELOP A PART | AR1980 | 774 |
| 1 A STATE1 . THIS1 ENACTMENT WILL1 ENABLE THE NEW1 | STATE1 | OF PUERTO RICO TO1 STAND1 ECONOMICALLY ON AN EQUA | AR1980 | 299 |
| AND EFFORTS TO1 RETURN1 DECISION-MAKING POWER1 TO1 | STATE1 | AND LOCAL ELECTED OFFICIAL1S . WE PLEDGE TO1 REV | AR1980 | 1021 |
| LP2 RETURN1 CONTROL1 OF WELFARE2 PROGRAM1S TO2 THE | STATE1S | . WE SUPPORT1 A BLOCK1 GRANT2 PROGRAM1 THAT2 WIL | AR1980 | 151 |
| SUE CLOSE1 TIE3S AND FRIENDSHIP WITH MODERATE ARAB | STATE1S | . WHILE2 REEMPHASIZING OUR COMMITMENT TO2 ISRAEL | AR1980 | 1411 |
| L4LING INFLUENCE1 OVER2 THE REGIONS' RESOURCE-RICH | STATE1S | . AND THEREBY TO1 GAIN1 DECISIVE POLITICAL AND | AR1980 | 1391 |
| AS3 LEFT3 THE U.S. ARMED1 FORCE2S AT THEIR LOW2EST | STATE2 | OF PREPAREDNESS SINCE1 1950 , SERICUSLY COMPROMIS | AR1980 | 1249 |
| OPMENT . ' IN OUR PLATFORM1 FOUR YEAR1S AGO , WE | STATE3D | THAT2 , ' THE GROWTH OF CIVILIAN NUCLEAR TECHN | AR1980 | 1319 |
| US TO1 CATCH4 UP . THE SECRETARY2 OF DEFENSE HAS3 | STATE3D | THAT3 , ' EVEN5 IF WE WERE1 TO1 MAINTAIN1 A CONSTANT | AR1980 | 1151 |
| THE MINIMUM QUANTITYIES THE ARMED1 SERVICE1S HAVE3 | STATE3D | THEY NEED1 . YET3 FUNDING REQUEST1S FOR SUFFICI | AR1980 | 1248 |

*(continued)*

49

# TABLE 3.2 Continued

## 1980 Carter Democratic Platform

| Left context | Keyword and right context | Source | Line |
|---|---|---|---|
| NCENTIVES TO1 MAKE1 ALL1 RESIDENCES IN THE UNITE2D | STATES ENERGY EFFICIENT , THROUGH2 UPGRADED INSULATION , | AD1980 | 1195 |
| ATION OF THE LEADERSHIP ROLE TAKEN1 BY THE UNITE2D | STATES IN THE AREA OF HUMAN RIGHT1S AND URGE1 THAT1 THE | AD1980 | 1576 |
| RE . WITH THOSE1 TREATYIES RATIFYIED , THE UNITE2D | STATES IN 1980 IS1 NOT ONLY2 IDENTIFYIED WITH THE CAUSE3 | AD1980 | 1762 |
| AL REGIME IN THE WEST BANK2 AND GAZA , THE UNITE2D | STATES IS1 A FULL1 PARTNER IN NEGOTIATIONS BETWEEN ISRAE | AD1980 | 1620 |
| COLLECTIVE DEFENSE EFFORTS . IN 1977 , THE UNITE2D | STATES JOIN2ED WITH NATO TO1 DEVELOP . FOR THE FIRST1 TI | AD1980 | 1455 |
| 2 TERM1S IN THE LAST1 THREE YEAR1S . THE UNITE2D | STATES NON-FARM EXPORT1S HAVE3 RISEN1 50 PERCENT IN REAL | AD1980 | 157 |
| AN ASSAULT1 ON THE VITAL INTEREST1S OF THE UNITE2D | STATES OF AMERICA AND SUCH1 AN ASSAULT1 WILL1 BE3 REPELL | AD1980 | 1495 |
| ASSISTANCE . IT IS1 UNACCEPTABLE THAT1 THE UNITE2D | STATES RANKS 13TH AMONG 17 MAJOR1 INDUSTRIAL POWER1S IN | AD1980 | 1733 |
| DING TO1 FERMENT IN THE THIRD1 WORLD . THE UNITE2D | STATES SHOULD BE1 A POSITIVE FORCE1 FOR PEACEFUL CHANGE2 | AD1980 | 1437 |
| PORT1S AND REDRESS TRADE1 IMBALANCES , THE UNITE2D | STATES SHOULD CONFORM WITH THE PRACTICE2S OF OTHER1 MAJO | AD1980 | 1029 |
| 18-YEAR-OLD S IS3 INTEND1ED TO1 ENABLE THE UNITE2D | STATES TO1 MOBILIZE MORE RAPID2LY IN THE EVENT3 OF AN EM | AD1980 | 1483 |
| N3 STRENGTHEN1ED . AT THE SAME TIME1 , THE UNITE2D | STATES' COMMITMENT TO2 THE INDEPENDENCE , SECURITY1 , AN | AD1980 | 1622 |
| OME COUNTRY1IES . WE WILL1 CONTRIBUTE1 THE UNITE2D | STATES' FAIR5 SHARE1 TO2 THE CAPITAL OF THE MULTILATERAL | AD1980 | 1736 |
| D1 TO2 ISRAEL SINCE1 ITS CREATION AS1 A SOVEREIGN | STATE1 - MORE THAN $10 BILLION - HAS3 BEEN3 REQUEST2ED D | AD1980 | 1630 |
| ICH ACTIVE2LY INVOLVE3D THE ELECT2ED OFFICIAL1S OF | STATE1 AND LOCAL GOVERNMENT , REPRESENTATIVE1S OF LABOR2 | AD1980 | 1623 |
| TION AND TREATMENT ACT1 WHICH PROVIDE1S TO1 | STATE1 AND COMMUNITY GROUP1S . AND - AMENDMENTS TO2 THE | AD1980 | 783 |
| F PROVIDE1ING IMMEDIATE1 FEDERAL FISCAL RELIEF TO1 | STATE1 AND LOCAL GOVERNMENTS . THE FEDERAL GOVERNMENT WI | AD1980 | 982 |
| HE OPPOSITE - TO1 PROVIDE1 GREAT3ER ASSISTANCE TO1 | STATE1 AND LOCAL GOVERNMENTS FOR THEIR WELFARE2 COST1S A | AD1980 | 550 |
| FICANT ADM1NISTRATIVE AND ORGANIZATIONAL ROLES FOR | STATE1 AND LOCAL GOVERNMENT IN SETTING POLICY AND IN RE | AD1980 | 569 |
| HE REGION . WE WILL1 JOIN2 WITH OTHER1 LIKE-MINDED | STATE1S IN PURSUEING HUMAN RIGHT1S , DEMOCRACY AND ECO | AD1980 | 371 |
| HE U . S . TERRITORY1IES AND OTHER1 EMERGE1ING ISLAND | STATE1S IN THE PACIFIC1 BASIN PLAY2 . THE SOLID1FICATIO | AD1980 | 1775 |
| BUILD1 A COMPREHENSIVE PEACE1 . WE CALL1 UPON ALL1 | STATE1S IN THE REGION TO1 SUPPORT1 THE HISTORIC EFFORTS | AD1980 | 1801 |
| M OUR SUPPORT2 FOR THE 1962 ACTION AND URGE1 THAT1 | STATE1S NOT PROVIDE1ING ASSISTANCE TO2 UNIFYIED FAMIL1YIE | AD1980 | 1639 |
| NATIONAL ECONOMIC1 PROSPERITY. OUR 1976 PLATFORM1 | STATE3D : EVEN2 DURING PERIODS OF NORMAL ECONOMIC1 GROWT | AD1980 | 129 |
| ITS HOLY PLACE1S PROVIDE1D TO2 ALL1 FAITH1S . AS1 | STATE3D IN THE 1976 PLATFORM2 , THE DEMOCRATIC PARTY2 RE | AD1980 | 1635 |
| OUS TO2 A BEAUTIFUL MOSAIC . PRESIDENT CARTER HAS3 | STATE3D THAT1 THE COMPOSITION OF AMERICAN1 SOCIETY IS1 A | AD1980 | 1008 |

**TABLE 3.3**

**Ordered Word Frequency Lists, 1976-1980 Democratic and Republican Presidential Platforms**

| Jimmy Carter, 1976 | | | Gerald Ford, 1976 | | | Jimmy Carter, 1980 | | | Ronald Reagan, 1980 | | |
|---|---|---|---|---|---|---|---|---|---|---|---|
| Rank | Word | Frequency | Rank | Word | Frequency | Rank | Word | Frequency | Rank | Word | Frequency |
| 1 | OUR | 222 | 1 | OUR | 318 | 1 | OUR | 430 | 1 | OUR | 347 |
| 2 | MUST | 140 | 2 | MUST | 148 | 2 | MUST | 321 | 2 | THEIR | 161 |
| 3 | SHOULD | 130 | 3 | SHOULD | 109 | 3 | DEMOCRATIC | 226 | 3 | ADMINISTRATION | 131 |
| 4 | DEMOCRATIC | 90 | 4 | GOVERNMENT | 100 | 4 | FEDERAL | 177 | 4 | GOVERNMENT | 128 |
| 5 | GOVERNMENT | 87 | 5 | STATES | 86 | 5 | SUPPORT | 144 | 5 | REPUBLICAN | 126 |
| 6 | ECONOMIC | 78 | 6 | FEDERAL | 75 | 6 | PARTY | 139 | 5 | FEDERAL | 126 |
| 6 | SUPPORT | 78 | 7 | UNITED | 74 | 7 | GOVERNMENT | 133 | 6 | AMERICAN | 119 |
| 7 | FEDERAL | 74 | 8 | SUPPORT | 73 | 8 | PROGRAMS | 129 | 7 | REPUBLICANS | 116 |
| 8 | ALL | 72 | 9 | ALL | 70 | 9 | ADMINISTRATION | 127 | 8 | CARTER | 112 |
| 9 | STATES | 69 | 10 | THEIR | 66 | 10 | ALL | 122 | 9 | MUST | 104 |
| 9 | UNITED | 69 | 11 | NATIONAL | 61 | 10 | ECONOMIC | 122 | 10 | ECONOMIC | 101 |
| 10 | POLICY | 67 | 12 | POLICY | 60 | 11 | THEIR | 112 | 11 | POLICY | 100 |
| 10 | PROGRAMS | 67 | 13 | AMERICAN | 56 | 12 | CONTINUE | 109 | 12 | SOVIET | 98 |
| 11 | PARTY | 66 | 14 | PROGRAMS | 52 | 13 | ENERGY | 107 | 13 | STATES | 93 |
| 12 | ENERGY | 62 | 15 | REPUBLICAN | 51 | 14 | SHOULD | 99 | 14 | MILITARY | 89 |
| 13 | NATIONAL | 59 | 16 | PEOPLE | 49 | 15 | OTHER | 96 | 15 | TAX | 85 |
| 14 | PUBLIC | 51 | 17 | CONGRESS | 48 | 16 | POLICY | 89 | 16 | SUPPORT | 83 |
| 15 | AMERICAN | 48 | 18 | WORLD | 46 | 17 | EFFORTS | 87 | 17 | ENERGY | 81 |
| 16 | PEOPLE | 47 | 19 | MORE | 45 | 17 | DEVELOPMENT | 87 | 17 | MORE | 81 |
| 17 | THEIR | 46 | 20 | SYSTEM | 44 | 18 | RIGHTS | 86 | 18 | PARTY | 79 |
| 18 | HEALTH | 45 | 21 | DEMOCRATIC | 43 | 19 | HEALTH | 85 | 19 | PEOPLE | 74 |
| 19 | OTHER | 44 | 22 | DEVELOPMENT | 42 | 20 | AMERICAN | 84 | 20 | UNITED | 73 |
| 20 | INTERNATIONAL | 43 | 23 | ECONOMIC | 41 | 21 | PROGRAM | 81 | 21 | PROGRAMS | 72 |
| 21 | DEVELOPMENT | 42 | 23 | ENERGY | 41 | 21 | MORE | 81 | 21 | THEY | 72 |
| 22 | NEEDS | 40 | 23 | OTHER | 41 | 22 | NATIONAL | 80 | 22 | ALL | 70 |
| 23 | POLICIES | 39 | 24 | THEY | 40 | 23 | NEW | 79 | 22 | POLICIES | 70 |
| 23 | TAX | 39 | 25 | NEW | 39 | 24 | STATES | 73 | 23 | AMERICANS | 68 |
| 24 | MORE | 38 | 26 | CONTINUE | 37 | 25 | SECURITY | 72 | 24 | SHOULD | 64 |
| 24 | SYSTEM | 38 | 27 | THROUGH | 36 | 26 | WOMEN | 70 | 25 | NEW | 63 |
| 25 | NEW | 37 | 28 | LOCAL | 35 | 27 | WORK | 69 | 26 | BELIEVE | 62 |
| 26 | ADMINISTRATION | 36 | 29 | AMERICANS | 33 | 28 | EDUCATION | 65 | 26 | DEFENSE | 62 |
| 26 | EFFORTS | 36 | 29 | NATIONS | 33 | 29 | YEARS | 64 | 26 | NATIONAL | 62 |
| 26 | WORLD | 36 | 29 | TAX | 33 | 30 | NEEDS | 62 | 26 | WHO | 62 |
| 27 | HOUSING | 34 | 30 | WORK | 32 | 30 | PEOPLE | 62 | 27 | PLEDGE | 61 |
| 28 | FULL | 33 | 31 | CARE | 30 | 31 | ALSO | 61 | 28 | FOREIGN | 60 |
| 29 | CITIZENS | 32 | 31 | FOREIGN | 30 | 32 | THEY | 60 | 29 | GROWTH | 58 |
| 30 | BOTH | 31 | 31 | MOST | 30 | 32 | WORLD | 60 | 30 | OTHER | 55 |
| 30 | FORCES | 31 | 31 | NOW | 30 | 33 | SOVIET | 58 | 31 | MOST | 53 |
| 30 | RIGHTS | 31 | 31 | SECURITY | 30 | 34 | HUMAN | 57 | 31 | SECURITY | 53 |
| 31 | AREAS | 30 | 32 | RESOURCES | 29 | 35 | PROVIDE | 56 | 32 | YEARS | 51 |
| 31 | PROVIDE | 30 | 32 | THERE | 29 | 35 | UNITED | 56 | 33 | THROUGH | 50 |
| 31 | SOCIAL | 30 | 32 | USE | 29 | 36 | INTERNATIONAL | 55 | 34 | INFLATION | 49 |
| 31 | WORK | 30 | 33 | RIGHTS | 28 | 36 | AREAS | 55 | 34 | PRIVATE | 49 |
| 31 | YEARS | 30 | 33 | SHALL | 28 | 36 | CARE | 55 | 35 | JOBS | 48 |

Comparison of the lists for the two 1976 platforms suggests that the Carter and Ford documents use similar words with about the same relative frequencies. For example, the two most frequent words in each platform are identical, and there are obvious similarities in the top ten words. Nevertheless, noticeable differences exist. "Economic" and "health" are ranked 6th and 18th in the Carter platform, yet in the Ford platform "economic" ranks only 23rd and "health" is not among the most frequent words.

Comparison between the 1976 and 1980 platform reveals striking differences. "Soviet," "military," and "defense" rank high in Reagan's platform but are not among the most frequent words in either of the 1976 platforms. "Soviet" ranks 33rd in the 1980 Carter platform but the other two words fail to make this short list. "Health," "women," and "education" rank high in the 1980 Carter document but are not among the high-frequency words in the Reagan document.

This table confirms that the Reagan platform articulated a very different set of priorities and concerns than either the Carter campaign or the previous Ford Republican platform. The relationship between articulations and actions remains to be thoroughly investigated. However, in a great many instances the Reagan administration promised policies that are a radical departure from the promised policies of the past. Similar data can be generated over long periods of time to allow study of the relationship between articulations, policy changes, and voter response.

Ordered word frequency lists provide a convenient way of getting at gross differences in word usage. Table 3.3 illustrates that these differences may be between the same message source at different points in time; different message sources at the same time; or both.

Several assumptions underlie this mode of analysis. One obvious assumption is that the most frequently appearing words reflect the greatest concerns. This is likely to be true generally but two cautions must be noted. First, one word may be used in a variety of contexts or may have more than one meaning, so that word frequencies may suggest far greater uniformity in usage than actually exists. This calls into question the validity of word frequency data. For instance, "states" appears frequently in all four platforms. One cannot tell from just the word frequency list whether the platform addresses states rights, the United States, sovereign states, or the state of affairs. However, to augment a word frequency list, a concordance can be used to assess the uniformity of word usage and to generate counts of specific phrases.

Second, the use of synonyms and/or pronouns for stylistic reasons may lead to the underestimation of actual concern with particular words or phrases. For example, in Democratic platforms the pronoun "we" may refer to the party or to an incumbent administration. If one were interested in counting self-references, perhaps the best index would be the sum of references to "we" in the former sense, the phrase "Democratic Party," and perhaps references to "our party." Thus simple counts of any one, rather than all of these words or phrases, will yield invalid indicators of self-reference. No simple resolution of this problem currently exists. Key-word-in-context lists discussed in the previous section do provide the basis for valid indicators of concepts such as party self-reference. However, for studies employing numerous indicators, this may be an impractical, time-consuming answer.[41]

The previous chapter noted the ability of some computer sofware to distinguish among words with more than one meaning or to treat

## TABLE 3.4
### Ordered Word Frequency Lists, 1976-1980 Democratic and Republican Presidential Party Platforms, Disambiguated Text

| Jimmy Carter, 1976 | | | Gerald Ford, 1976 | | | Jimmy Carter, 1980 | | | Ronald Reagan, 1980 | | |
|---|---|---|---|---|---|---|---|---|---|---|---|
| Rank | Word | Frequency | Rank | Word | Frequency | Rank | Word | Frequency | Rank | Word | Frequency |
| 1 | OUR | 222 | 1 | OUR | 318 | 1 | OUR | 430 | 1 | OUR | 347 |
| 2 | MUST1 | 140 | 2 | MUST1 | 148 | 2 | MUST1 | 321 | 2 | THEIR | 161 |
| 3 | SHOULD | 130 | 3 | SHOULD | 109 | 3 | DEMOCRATIC | 226 | 3 | GOVERNMENT | 128 |
| 4 | DEMOCRATIC | 90 | 4 | GOVERNMENT | 100 | 4 | FEDERAL | 177 | 4 | FEDERAL | 126 |
| 5 | GOVERNMENT | 87 | 5 | FEDERAL | 75 | 5 | GOVERNMENT | 133 | 4 | REPUBLICAN | 126 |
| 6 | ECONOMIC1 | 78 | 6 | THEIR | 67 | 6 | PROGRAMS | 129 | 5 | ADMINISTRATION1 | 125 |
| 7 | FEDERAL | 74 | 7 | STATES | 65 | 7 | ADMINISTRATION1 | 124 | 6 | AMERICAN1 | 117 |
| 8 | POLICY | 67 | 7 | UNITE2D | 65 | 8 | ECONOMIC1 | 122 | 7 | REPUBLICANS | 116 |
| 8 | PROGRAMS | 67 | 8 | NATIONAL | 61 | 9 | PARTY2 | 116 | 8 | CARTER | 112 |
| 9 | PARTY1 | 66 | 9 | POLICY | 60 | 10 | THEIR | 112 | 9 | MUST1 | 104 |
| 10 | ENERGY | 62 | 10 | AMERICAN1 | 56 | 11 | CONTINUE1 | 109 | 10 | ECONOMIC1 | 101 |
| 11 | ALL1 | 59 | 11 | ALL1 | 53 | 12 | ENERGY | 107 | 11 | POLICY | 100 |
| 11 | NATIONAL | 59 | 12 | PROGRAMS | 52 | 13 | ALL1 | 106 | 12 | SOVIET | 98 |
| 12 | UNITE2D | 55 | 13 | REPUBLICAN | 51 | 14 | SHOULD | 99 | 13 | MILITARY | 89 |
| 13 | STATES | 54 | 14 | PEOPLE1 | 49 | 15 | OTHER1 | 96 | 14 | ENERGY | 81 |
| 14 | PEOPLE1 | 47 | 15 | WORLD | 46 | 16 | POLICY | 89 | 14 | MORE | 81 |
| 15 | AMERICAN1 | 46 | 16 | MORE | 45 | 17 | DEVELOPMENT | 87 | 15 | TAX1 | 80 |
| 15 | THEIR | 46 | 16 | SUPPORT1 | 45 | 17 | EFFORTS | 87 | 16 | PEOPLE1 | 74 |
| 16 | HEALTH | 45 | 17 | SYSTEM | 44 | 18 | HEALTH | 85 | 17 | PROGRAMS | 73 |
| 17 | PUBLIC1 | 44 | 18 | DEMOCRATIC | 43 | 19 | AMERICAN1 | 84 | 18 | THEY | 72 |
| 18 | INTERNATIONAL1 | 43 | 19 | DEVELOPMENT | 42 | 20 | MORE | 81 | 19 | POLICYIES | 70 |
| 19 | DEVELOPMENT | 42 | 20 | ECONOMIC1 | 41 | 20 | PROGRAM1 | 81 | 20 | UNITE2D | 69 |
| 19 | OTHER | 42 | 20 | ENERGY | 41 | 21 | NATIONAL | 80 | 21 | AMERICAN1S | 68 |
| 20 | SUPPORT1 | 41 | 21 | THEY | 40 | 22 | NEW1 | 79 | 22 | STATES | 67 |
| 21 | POLICYIES | 39 | 22 | CONGRESS1 | 38 | 23 | SUPPORT1 | 75 | 23 | SHOULD | 64 |
| 22 | MORE | 38 | 22 | NEW1 | 38 | 25 | SUPPORT2 | 72 | 24 | DEFENSE | 62 |
| 22 | THESE1 | 38 | 23 | CONTINUE1 | 37 | 25 | WOMEN | 72 | 24 | NATIONAL | 62 |
| 22 | SYSTEM | 38 | 23 | OTHER1 | 37 | 26 | EDUCATION | 65 | 24 | NEW1 | 62 |
| 22 | TAX1 | 38 | 24 | LOCAL | 35 | 26 | RIGHT1S | 65 | 24 | WHO | 62 |
| 23 | SUPPORT2 | 37 | 25 | AMERICAN1S | 33 | 27 | YEAR1S | 64 | 25 | BELIEVE1 | 61 |
| 23 | NEW1 | 37 | 25 | NATIONS | 33 | 28 | PEOPLE1 | 62 | 25 | PLEDGE | 61 |
| 24 | EFFORTS | 36 | 26 | TAX1 | 31 | 29 | ALSO | 61 | 26 | FOREIGN1 | 60 |
| 24 | WORLD | 36 | 27 | FOREIGN1 | 30 | 30 | THEY | 60 | 27 | ALL1 | 59 |
| 25 | HOUSE4ING | 34 | 27 | NOW | 30 | 30 | WORLD | 60 | 28 | GROWTH | 58 |
| 26 | FULL1 | 33 | 28 | RESOURCES | 29 | 31 | SOVIET | 58 | 29 | PARTY3 | 56 |
| 26 | ADMINISTRATION1 | 33 | 28 | THROUGH2 | 29 | 32 | HUMAN | 57 | 30 | MOST1 | 51 |
| 27 | CITIZENS | 32 | 29 | RIGHT1S | 28 | 33 | PROVIDE1 | 56 | 30 | YEAR1S | 51 |
| 28 | AREAS | 30 | 30 | INTERNATIONAL1 | 27 | 34 | AREAS | 55 | 31 | OTHER1 | 50 |
| 28 | NEED2S | 30 | 31 | COMMUNITY | 26 | 34 | CARE1 | 55 | 31 | SUPPORT1 | 50 |
| 28 | YEAR1S | 30 | 31 | HEALTH | 26 | 34 | INTERNATIONAL1 | 55 | 32 | INFLATION | 49 |
| 28 | PROVIDE1 | 30 | 31 | PARTY1 | 26 | 34 | PERCENT | 55 | 32 | PRIVATE1 | 49 |
| 28 | EMPLOYMENT | 30 | 31 | PROVIDE1 | 26 | 35 | NEED2S | 54 | 33 | JOBS | 48 |
| 29 | REPUBLICAN | 29 | 32 | TAXIN | 25 | 36 | ASSISTANCE | 51 | 33 | PERCENT | 48 |
| 29 | MILITARY | 29 | | | | 36 | RESOURCES | 51 | 33 | SYSTEM | 48 |

phrases as a single semantic unit. Table 3.4 presents ordered word frequency lists for the 1976 and 1980 party platforms based on disambiguated text. "Support," for example, moves from 5th to 23rd and 25th in the 1980 Carter platform. The first sense of "support" is the verb form, and the second sense is the noun form, meaning sustain, provide for, or encouragement, as in "The bill has our support." However, the ranking of most words does not change greatly. Consequently, the overall conclusions would not be different as a result of disambiguation. But because the text classification procedure is more precise, the data in this table have greater semantic validity than the data in the previous table.

Although word frequency lists reveal changes or differences in emphasis between documents, they must be used with caution. Word frequencies do not reveal very much about the associations among words. For example, although it may be interesting to know that "support" ranks higher in the 1980 Carter platform than in the 1980

Reagan platform, this does not reveal whether they differ in their support of democractic principles, the equal rights amendment, or foreign countries that have pro-Western authoritatian regimes. Having used ordered word frequency lists to identify words of potential interest, the investigator should use KWIC lists or retrievals from text to investigate and understand the larger context of symbol usage.

## Retrievals from Coded Text

Another important benefit of computer-aided content analysis is that the investigator may easily search[42] through the text to retrieve portions meeting specific criteria (compare Ogilvie, 1966; Stone et al., 1966; 121ff). One way of searching text is to retrieve sentences based on the occurrence of at least one word in a particular category, for example, all sentences with one Wealth word. Some investigators (DeWeese, personal communication) strongly feel that counts and retrievals based on the co-occurrence[43] (or combination) of categories or words in a single sentence are the most useful indicators. Of course, one difficulty is knowing which combinations will be particularly useful. Presumably, substantive hypotheses suggest appropriate combinations, but induction usually prevails. Another difficulty in analyzing co-occurrences is that some combinations that might be of substantive interest may occur relatively infrequently. In the social science literature there is little, if any, systematic research on retrievals; hence, only a brief example will be given.

Using party platforms from 1844 to 1864, the computer was instructed to retrieve all sentences with at least one Wealth word that was a noun and that also had any word in the category Well-Being-Deprivation. The latter category indicates a concern with the loss of well-being, either of a person or a collectivity. Table 3.5 presents a sample of nine sentences meeting this criteria.[44] The criterion words are underscored. The program retrieved sentences addressing two different subjects. Some sentences mention economic difficulties; others mention pensions for the survivors of the war dead and for the disabled. Sentence 3 contains both themes.

Obviously, the diversity of sentences retrieved can be narrowed or expanded by varying the criteria of selection: More criteria will result in fewer retrievals; fewer criteria will result in more. But the primary difficulty is that the results depend upon an interaction between the text, the category scheme, and the assignment of words to categories. Thus

# TABLE 3.5

## Selected Retrievals, Democratic and Republican Platforms, Sentences With Wealth Nouns and Well-Being-Deprivation, 1844-1964

DOC# 12   SENT# 12   ID=D1868
AND A TARIFF FOR REVENUE UPON FOREIGN1 IMPORTS, SUCH2 AS WILL2 AFFORD1 INCIDENTAL PROTECTION TO2 DOMESTIC MANUFACTURE1S, AND AS1 WILL1 WITHOUT IMPAIRING THE REVENUE, IMPOSE THE LEAST2 BURDEN1 UPON, AND BEST PROMOTE AND ENCOURAGE1 THE GREAT1 INDUSTRIAL INTERESTS OF THE COUNTRY1 .
*** END DOCUMENT, NUMBER RETRIEVALS=   1

DOC# 18   SENT# 23   ID=R1872
THEIR PENSIONS ARE1 A SACRED DEBT OF THE NATION, AND THE WIDOW1S AND ORPHANS OF THOSE2 WHO DIED FOR THEIR COUNTRY1 ARE3 ENTITLED TO2 THE CARE1 OF A GENEROUS AND GRATEFUL PEOPLE1 .
*** END DOCUMENT, NUMBER RETRIEVALS=   1

DOC# 22   SENT# 16   ID=R1880
AND THAT1 THE LIBERTY SECURE1D TO2 THIS1 GENERATION SHOULD BE3 TRANSMITTED UNDIMINISHED TO2 OTHER1 GENERATIONS, THAT1 THE ORDER2 ESTABLISHED AND THE CREDIT1 ACQUIRE2D SHOULD NEVER BE3 IMPAIRED, THAT1 THE PENSIONS PROMISE2D SHOULD BE3 PAID1, THAT1 THE DEBT SO1 MUCH REDUCED SHOULD BE3 EXTINGUISHED BY THE FULL1 PAYMENT OF EVERY DOLLAR .
*** END DOCUMENT, NUMBER RETRIEVALS=   1

DOC# 24   SENT# 31   ID=R1884
THE GRATEFUL THANK2S OF THE AMERICAN PEOPLE1 ARE1 DUE1 TO2 THE UNION1 SOLDIERS AND SAILORS OF THE LATE2 WAR1 AND THE REPUBLICAN PARTY1 STAND1S PLEDGED TO2 SUITABLE PENSIONS FOR ALL2 WHO WERE3 DISABLED, AND FOR THE WIDOW1S AND ORPHANS OF THOSE2 WHO DIED IN THE WAR1 .

DOC# 24   SENT# 33   ID=R1884
SO2 THAT1 ALL1 INVALID SOLDIERS SHALL SHARE1 ALIKE, AND THEIR PENSIONS BEGIN1 WITH THE DATE1 OF DISABILITY OR DISCHARGE1, AND NOT WITH THE DATE1 OF APPLICATION .
*** END DOCUMENT, NUMBER RETRIEVALS=   2

DOC# 29   SENT# 50   ID=D1896
RECOGNIZING THE JUST3 CLAIM1S OF DESERVING UNION1 SOLDIERS, WE HEARTILY INDORSE THE RULE1 OF THE PRESENT1 COMMISSIONER OF PENSIONS THAT1 NO1 NAME1S SHALL BE3 ARBITRARYLY DROP3PED FROM THE PENSION ROLL1 AND THE FACT1 OF ENLISTMENT AND SERVICE1 SHOULD BE3 DEEMED CONCLUSIVE EVIDENCE1 AGAINST DISEASE AND DISABILITY BEFORE ENLISTMENT .
*** END DOCUMENT, NUMBER RETRIEVALS=   1

DOC# 30   SENT# 21   ID=R1896
WE BELIEVE1 THE REPEAL OF THE RECIPROCITY ARRANGEMENTS NEGOTIATED BY THE LAST1 REPUBLICAN ADMINISTRATION1 WAS1 A NATIONAL CALAMITY, AND DEMAND2 THEIR RENEWAL AND EXTENSION ON SUCH1 TERM3S AS1 WILL1 EQUALIZE OUR TRADE1 WITH OTHER1 NATIONS, REMOVE THE RESTRICTIONS WHICH NOW OBSTRUCT THE SALE OF AMERICAN PRODUCT1S IN THE PORTS OF OTHER1 COUNTRY1IES+

DOC# 30   SENT# 35   ID=R1896
WE ARE3 UNALTERABLELY OPPOSE2D TO2 EVERY MEASURE1 CALCULATE2D TO1 DEBASE OUR CURRENCY OR IMPAIR THE CREDIT1 OF OUR COUNTRY1 .
*** END DOCUMENT, NUMBER RETRIEVALS=   3

DOC# 31   SENT# 67   ID=D1900
WE ARE1 PROUD OF THE COURAGE AND FIDELITY OF THE AMERICAN SOLDIERS AND SAILORS IN ALL1 OUR WAR1S, WE FAVOR2 LIBERAL2 PENSION1S TO2 THEM AND THEIR DEPENDENTS AND WE REITERATE THE POSITION1 TAKEN1 IN THE CHICAGO PLATFORM2 OF 1896 THAT1 THE FACT1 OF ENLISTMENT AND SERVICE1 SHALL BE3 DEEMED CONCLUSIVE EVIDENCE1 AGAINST DISEASE AND DISABILITY BEFORE ENLISTMENT .
*** END DOCUMENT, NUMBER RETRIEVALS=   1

each investigator will have to experiment with retrievals in order to find the approach most helpful to her or his goals. No general guidelines exist.

Finally, why use retrievals based on categories? Why not use retrievals based on words? Certainly the computer is capable of doing either. For example, one could retrieve all sentences containing the words "pension" or "pensions." However, this might retrieve some sentences dealing with the pensions of postal workers. Instead, sentences with "pension" and "disability" could be retrieved, but this would miss sentence 2 in Table 3.5, which is similar in content to the others dealing with pensions for veterans and their survivors. Synonyms are frequently used that would be missed by a purely word-oriented approach to retrievals, but they are easily captured in a category-based system.

## Category Counts

Another approach to analyzing text is based on counting words that have been classified into categories. As noted above, counting is based on the assumption that higher relative counts (proportions, percentages, or ranks) reflect higher concern with the category.

Counting is often useful because it may reveal aspects of the text that otherwise would not be apparent. For instance, one substantive question arises in the analysis of party platforms: Over time, how do the Democrats and Republicans vary with respect to each other in their concerns? Figure 3.1 indicates each party's concern with Wealth-Total 1844-1980.[45] For each party, the data consist of the percent of words in each platform categorized in Wealth-Total.[46]

Between 1844 and about 1952 there is a general rise in the percentage of each platform devoted to economic matters (Figure 3.1). This increase probably reflects the greater importance of the state in the management of economic affairs. Second, from 1952 or so to the present, there is a relatively constant level of concern with economic matters. Third, and more important, since 1844 the nature of competition between the parties has changed qualitatively in dramatic ways.[47] From 1844 to 1894 (the left vertical reference line) the parties have varied opposite to each other in their concern with economic matters. Between 1896 and 1952 (the right vertical reference line) the parties manifest similar levels of economic concerns. However, between 1952 and 1980 they move opposite each other again, although the overall variation in

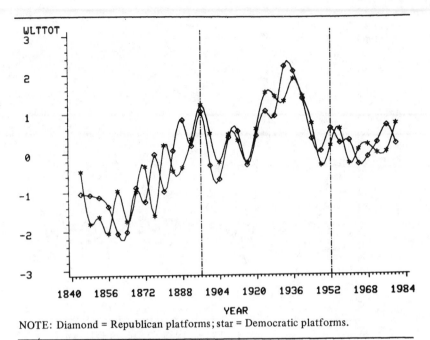

NOTE: Diamond = Republican platforms; star = Democratic platforms.

Figure 3.1: Democratic and Republican Concern with Wealth-Total, 1844-1980

this time period is relatively small. The break-points of 1894 and 1952 are congruent with Burnham's (1970) and others' interpretations of periodic realignments of the American party system (see Weber, 1982).

Not only may simple counts reveal differences between senders of the message, but they may also indicate how one message sources varies over time. For the Democratic party, Figure 3.2 illustrates how party platforms vary with respect to first person plural pronouns (Selves) and third person plural pronouns (Others). As might be expected, these categories vary inversely with each other: When the Democrats emphasize their own accomplishments and programs they de-emphasize those of the opposition. For Republican platforms, similar results were found (figure not shown here).

Even though these examples are drawn from political sociology, comparing simple percentages has been used in other realms to great advantage. For example, Aries (1973, 1977) analyzed conversations in small groups in order to make inferences about sex-role differences in group interactions (see Chapter 1 for a summary).

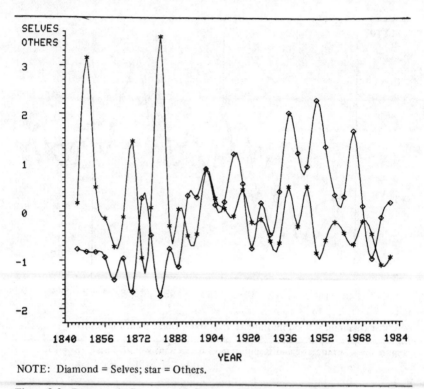

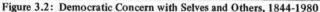

NOTE: Diamond = Selves; star = Others.

Figure 3.2: Democratic Concern with Selves and Others, 1844-1980

## Measurement Models

Although the preceding methods often work quite well, various investigators have employed multivariate data analysis techniques such as factor analysis[48] to identify themes in texts. Iker (1974; Iker and Harway, 1965, 1969), for example, factor-analyzed word frequency counts. Another approach (Namenwirth, 1969a; 1970; Namenwirth and Bibbee, 1975; Weber and Namenwirth, 1984a; forthcoming) applies factor analysis to category counts in order to identify themes in texts.[49] This section reports some of the factor analysis results in a study of American and British newspaper editorials (Namenwrith and Bibbee, 1975) and then considers interpretive problems. The next section outlines and critiques the substantive results based on the themes described here.

Using the General Inquirer computer systemn (Stone et al., 1966) and the Namenwirth Political Dictionary[50] (Namenwirth, n.d.), 288 randomly selected editorials concerning the Korean War from mass (New York *Daily News*, Boston *Daily Record*, and Washington *Daily News*) and elite (*New York Times, Christian Science Monitor,* and *Washington Post*) newspapers were content analyzed. For each editorial the computer reported the percentage of words in each of 40 categories retained for analysis.[51] Principal components analysis[52] produced four interpretable factors (accounting for 33% of the total variance). Table 3.6 presents for each category their factor loadings on the first two factors. These numbers may be interpreted as the correlation between the category and the factor. (Loadings $< |.30|$ are omitted.)

A group of categories that correlate (load on) the same factor tend to vary together and are interpreted as representing a theme in the text. For example, editorials that have frequent references to American leaders and topics (American) will also contain frequent references to words with higher status connotations (Higher Status) and occupational references (Job Role). Other editorials manifest concern with International Institutions, conciliatory feelings and moods (Approach), words implying interpersonal acceptance (Sign Accept), words connoting alarm or concern with danger (Danger Theme), and words concerned with maintaining the status quo (Static).

What do these themes mean or signify, and how can the investigator validate their interpretation? A discussion of factor interpretation is beyond the scope of this section. However, some practical guidelines may be helpful. For each editorial, the factor analysis procedure computes a score for each factor or theme. To determine if the themes identified in the factor analysis are real rather than statistical artifacts, three steps should be taken. As a first step, the analyst should examine those editorials that have the highest positive and the highest negative scores. Typically, texts with similar factor scores manifest similar concerns. Second, the analyst should examine how the words in these texts are classified. There should be many words classified in the categories that have high loadings on the factor. Third, the analyst should compare the texts with extreme positive and negative factor scores with each other and with texts that have scores of nearly zero for that theme. These contrasts should indicate that texts with high positive scores are quite different in content from those with zero scores, and that they are in some sense opposite to those with high negative scores.

Each factor can be thought of as representing a controversy of some sort. The themes at the positive and negative poles are typically opposing resolutions of this controversy. Examination of editorials with

**TABLE 3.6**
### Selected Themes in Korean War Editorials in Mass and Prestige Newspapers

Theme 1: Control of the Social Environment
Parochial versus Cosmopolitan

| Parochial Categories | Loadings | Cosmopolitan Categories | Loadings* |
|---|---|---|---|
| American | .85 | International institution | −.53 |
| Higher status | .80 | Approach | −.44 |
| Job role | .79 | Sign accept | −.42 |
| Male role | .68 | Danger theme | −.34 |
| Selves | .43 | Static | −.32 |
| Sign authority | .35 | | |

Theme 2: Control of the Physical Environment
Economic versus Military

| Economic Categories | Loadings | Military Categories | Loadings |
|---|---|---|---|
| Sign authority | .68 | Death theme | −.44 |
| Collective static | .64 | Social place | −.33 |
| Action norm | .55 | Natural world | −.31 |
| Guide | .47 | | |
| Ought | .46 | | |
| Control | .45 | | |
| Ideal value | .41 | | |
| Work | .40 | | |
| Individual static | .39 | | |
| Collective dynamic | .35 | | |
| Sign accept | .35 | | |
| Economic | .31 | | |
| Technological | .30 | | |

NOTE: Adapted from Namenwirth and Bibbee (1975) with permission.
*Loadings < |.30| are omitted.

extreme positive and negative scores on Factor 1 suggested to Namenwirth and Bibbee (1975) that this controversy addresses control of the social environment. Editorials propose two alternative solutions, which they label Parochial versus Cosmopolitan. The Parochial theme "stresses a fortress America stance: nationalism and isolationism best serve American interests and world peace," as illustrated by this excerpt from the Boston *Daily Record*, May 4, 1951, entitled "Now Let Us Have Facts":

> More than 10,500 Americans are dead in Korea because these three men (Truman, Acheson, and Marshall)[53] had a vested interest in their own mistakes. . . . Our concern is our sons in Korea. We frankly do not want any more Americans to die on that Asian peninsula seven thousand miles away from our shores, to protect the synthetic reputations of Acheson and Truman. Our sole concern is America and Americans. And that, we truly believe, is the concern of 99 percent of the American people [Namenwirth and Bibbee, 1975: 53].

The Cosmopolitan theme emphasizes "the need for an active role in world affairs, urging constant diplomatic initiative, coordination, and conciliation" (Namenwirth and Bibbee, 1975: 53), as illustrated by this excerpt from the December 3, 1952 *Christian Science Monitor* editorial entitled "Unity in the UN":

> To the (anti-communists) the (communist rejection of the Indian Truce Plan) should suggest the possibility of considerable strain between Moscow and Peking on this matter, a strain which free world diplomacy may exploit to advantage in the future. . . . It would be a great mistake for the anti-communist world to ignore the possibility (of future Chinese independence from Moscow), as it would be unrealistic for the neutral world to expect too much from it too soon. . . . Meanwhile the precarious unity of the non-communist countries, as shown in the UN vote, can best be maintained as the United States demonstrates how far it is from seeking to dominate its friends and allies in the iron-fisted Moscow manner [Namenwirth and Bibbee, 1975: 54].

The second issue or theme (Table 3.6) concerns contrasting approaches to control of the physical environment: Some editorials stress economic problems while other editorials stress military problems. Economic concerns mainly address inflation and the government's instituting and administering of a wartime system of price controls. Several categories correlate positively with this factor: normative patterns of social behavior (Action Norm); social-emotional actions consisting of assistance and positive direction (Guide); words indicating a moral imperative (Ought); words about limiting action (Control); task activity (Work); culturally defined virtues, goals, valued conditions, and activities (Ideal Value); the Economic and Technological rules, actions, and contexts,[54]" concern with the maintenance of the status quo, with the collectivity as agent or object of preferred action (Collective Static); and the same as the former, but indicating a concern with the change of the status quo (Collective Dynamic)."

The Economic theme is illustrated by this portion of the August 16, 1950 *Washington Post* editorial entitled "Defense Organization":

> The limited authority (Truman) has requested to allocate scarce materials, give priority to defense orders, tighten credit controls, and increase taxes certainly does not require any additional control machinery.... For the present, the existing organizational setup seems adequate to establish effective controls over allocations of the limited number of raw materials in short supply.... However much we may dislike the prospect, any effective general control over prices and living costs would necessitate the creation of a huge bureaucratic agency comparable to the Office of Price Administration. The government would also need new agencies to settle labor disputes, control and adjust wages [Namenwirth and Bibbee, 1975: 55].

Editorials manifesting the opposing theme are mainly concerned with the cost of military intervention in terms of wounded and mutilated soldiers (Death Theme) and military solutions for these emergencies. These problem solutions are also seen as part of nature rather than society (Social Place, Natural World). The following passage, from an editorial entitled "Saving the Wounded" that appeared in the April 5, 1952 *New York Times* illustrates this military theme:

> Good news from the Korean battle front was reported in a recent address in Los Angeles by Major General George E. Armstrong, Army Surgeon General. He said that United States soldiers, wounded in Korea, who reach hospitals near the front had more than twice as good a chance of recovery as did soldiers wounded in the Second World War. The medical corps, which has always been long on good hard work and short on publicity, warrants special commendation for this record. General Armstrong indicated that although body armor experiments had been favorable, teamwork between the medical corps, rescue troops, and helicopters had been an important factor in the diminishing death rate.

The essential point is that interpretations of statistical manipulations based on quantified text *must* be validated by reference to the text itself.

Examination of exemplary texts, here identified by extreme factor scores, will provide direct evidence for the interpretation. Similar themes in those editorials with similar extreme factor scores provide direct textual evidence that the same "story" is found repeatedly in a subset of texts, and consequently, that the results are not artifacts of the content classification or statistical techniques employed.

Examination of the texts may indicate the need to revise or discard the interpretation of the factor. Note that interpretation is in part an art. Those who naively believe that data or texts speak for themselves (the doctrine of radical empiricism) are mistaken. The content analyst contributes factual and theoretical knowledge to the interpretation, a topic taken up in Chapter 4.

The goal of content analysis cannot be just interpretation. Krippendorff (1980), for example, is right to stress that the content of texts, however interpreted, must be related either to the context that produced them or to some consequent state of affairs. The following section relates variation in the two sets of themes identified by Namenwirth and Bibbee (1975) to the type of newspaper in which they appeared.

**Accounting for Content 1:**
**Characteristics of the Message Producers**

As evidence of validity, many content analysis studies rely on internal consistency—showing that the textual evidence is consistent with the interpretation. Even when explanations are offered, it is seldom determined how strongly content-analytic variables are related to external factors. Using the two themes discussed just above, this section presents additional results indicating that variation in these themes depends in part upon characteristics of the message source (newspapers).

Namenwirth and Bibbee (1975) used an analysis of variance design[55] to assess the effect of newspaper type (elite/mass) on variation in themes, while simultaneously controlling for city (Boston, New York, or Washington) and time period during the Korean War.[56]

As Table 3.7 indicates, type of newspaper accounts for substantial variation in concern with Control of the Social Environment and Control of the Physical Environment—77% and 38%, respectively. Mass newspapers stress Parochial themes; prestige newspapers stress Cosmopolitan ones. In addition, the mass press stresses Military themes, and the prestige press stresses Economic problems. This result may not be surprising, because few sons of the elite classes were dying in Korea and because economic problems and controls directly affected the economic basis of the elite classes and their institutions.

### TABLE 3.7
### Prestige versus Mass Newspapers as a Determinant
### of Selected Themes in Editorials

Factor 1: Control of the Social Environment

| | Mass Newspapers | Prestige Newspapers |
|---|---|---|
| Mean factor score: | 1.56 | −1.56 |

F = 112.70; df = 1,270; p < .05; $\omega^2$ (%) = 77

Factor 2: Control of the Physical Environment

| | Mass Newspapers | Prestige Newspapers |
|---|---|---|
| Mean factor score: | −.75 | .75 |

F = 20.21; df = 1,270; p < .05; $\omega^2$ (%) = 38

NOTE: Adapted from Namenwirth and Bibbee (1975) with permission.

The amount of variance in the dependent variables explained by type of newspaper is much larger than in most studies not based on time-series analysis (econometricians routinely account for 90+ percent of the variance in the dependent variable). It should be noted that two other themes reported by Namenwirth and Bibbee (1975) did less well: type of newspaper accounted for only 15 percent and 6 percent of the variance, respectively. In addition, not all of the variance of the first two themes was accounted for by type of newspaper. This means, first, that other causes of newspaper content were not included in the design and hence not controlled. Second, some variance was accounted for by the two control variables, city and time. Third, error variance was not excluded from the factor scores,[57] and some unreliability remains.[58] This unreliability attenuates the relationship between themes and other variables.

## Accounting for Content 2:
## Changes in the Socioeconomic System

One of the most interesting and important applications of content analysis may be in cross-language designs. This section briefly describes recent findings from a pilot study undertaken to assess the cross-language validity of one major content-analysis dictionary. This research is being conducted by Professor Hans-Dieter Klingemann at the Freie Universitat Berlin, Peter Mohler of ZUMA, in Mannheim, and this writer. A detailed report will be published in the near future (Klingemann et al., in progress); hence, only a brief summary is given here.

The development of valid and reliable content-analytic instruments for the analysis of German language text is a prerequisite for studying quantitatively the relationships between changes in symbol usage, economy, society, and polity in German- and English-speaking countries. Consequently, the investigators carried out a pilot study to evaluate the cross-language validity and reliability of some content categories from the Lasswell Value Dictionary (Lasswell and Namenwirth, 1968; Namenwirth and Weber, 1984). Their immediate empirical question concerned the relationship between concern with wealth in the speeches of the kaiser from 1871 to 1912 and economic fluctuations.

Specifically, they hypothesized two theoretical concepts: "wealth concerns" and "economic performance." Each of these unobserved or latent variables is measured by two or more observed variables. Three Wealth categories of the Lasswell Value Dictionary measure wealth concerns: Wealth-Participants, Wealth-Transactions, and Wealth-Other. As noted in Chapter 2, the first category contains the names of those persons or positions involved in the creation, maintenance, and transfer of wealth, such as "banker." The Transactions category contains references to exchanges of wealth, such as "buying," "selling," and "borrowing." The Wealth-Other category contains wealth-related words not classified in the other two categories.

The measurement of economic performance in the period from 1871 to 1912 is difficult because reasonably valid and reliable economic data from this period are usually lacking. The investigators were fortunate, however, to locate the prices of wheat and rye on the Berlin wholesale grain market between 1871 and 1912. Grain prices have two qualities important for the purposes of the study. First, they are public information well known to most people, either directly, or indirectly through the price of bread and other grain products. Second, grain prices are likely to be less subject to measurement errors than are composite price indices or national accounts data based on aggregation across many units, such as estimates of Gross National Product. Although there may have been some regional variation in grain prices, the investigators believe that these data accurately represent the prices of two widely used commodities.

But what is the relationship between grain prices and economic performance? Prices are positively related to economic performance; that is, the price of grain and the economy tend to rise and fall together because price levels are in part an indicator of the inflation that often occurs in expanding economies. It is certainly true that other factors, such as weather, foreign trade, and the availability of substitutes, influence prices. However, only that part of variation in wheat and rye prices which the two variables have in common is used in the composite measure of economic performance. The remaining variance in wheat and rye prices is considered to be error variance consisting of measurement errors and variance due to factors other than economic performance.

If grain prices are an indicator of economic performance, then what is the relationship between economic performance and wealth concerns? Previous analyses of American and British political documents and economic change (Namenwirth 1969b, 1973; Weber 1981) indicate that economic performance and wealth concerns are inversely related: As the economy improves there is less concern with wealth; a declining economy is associated with increasing wealth concerns. In short, higher levels of concern with economic matters are associated with economic adversity. Anticipating the results, the data indicate a negative relationship between economic performance and wealth concerns in the speeches of the kaiser (1871-1912)—changes in the rate of change of the economy (acceleration) are negatively related to wealth concerns.[59]

Figure 3.3 indicates the structure of the causal model and the parameters to be estimated from the data. These unknown parameters (coefficients) are estimated using the LISREL approach to the analysis of covariance structures (Joreskog and Sorbom, 1979, 1984). The general LISREL model consists of two parts: the measurement model and the structural equation model. The measurement model indicates how latent or unobserved variables are related to observed variables. The structural equation model specifies the causal relationships among latent variables and indicates the causal effects and unexplained variance. In the model proposed above, the observed variables are content categories and the latent variables are economic performance and wealth concerns.

In addition to estimating the measurement and structural equation models simultaneously, the LISREL model also indicates how well the predicted covariance matrix reproduces or fits the observed covariance (or correlation) matrix. This indicator is an approximation to chi square with appropriate degrees of freedom for the number of free and

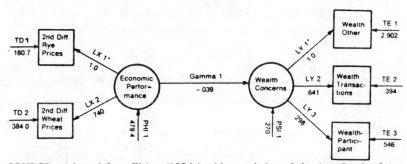

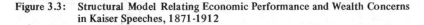

SOURCE: Adapted from Weber (1984a) with permission of the Austrian Academy of Sciences.
NOTE: $R^2 = .730$.
*Indicates fixed parameter.

**Figure 3.3:** Structural Model Relating Economic Performance and Wealth Concerns in Kaiser Speeches, 1871-1912

constrained parameters. The lower the chi square, the better the fit of the model to the data.

Table 3.8 and Figure 3.3 present the results.[60] Some caution is necessary in the interpretation of these results because the LISREL goodness-of-fit statistics assume large sample sizes. The chi square for the overall fit of the model is not significant (.905 with 4 df, $p < .9238$), which indicates that there is a very small probability of finding a better fitting model. Almost all the estimated parameters are twice their standard errors. The t statistic for the causal coefficient between economic performance and wealth concerns is just under 2, at 1.98. In addition, the t statistic for the error variance of the dependent variable (wealth concerns) is .667, which in this case indicates that there is very little error variance left (that is, the residual or error variance is not different from zero). This is not surprising as economic performance accounts for 73% of the variance in wealth concerns. The coefficient indicating the loading of Wealth-Participants on wealth concerns (LY3) is not significant, but given the overall results of the model and the relatively low number of cases the researchers decided to leave this variable in the model.

Finally, the magnitude and direction of the relationship between wealth concerns and economic performance indicates that the Wealth categories the investigators constructed for German text are quite

TABLE 3.8
### LISREL Parameter Estimates: Economic Performance and Wealth Concerns in Kaiser Speeches, 1871-1912*

| Parameter | Unstandard Coefficient | Standard Error | t |
|---|---|---|---|
| LX1** | 1.000 | | |
| LX2 | .740 | .275 | 2.690 |
| TD1 | 180.700 | 155.100 | 1.165 |
| TD2 | 384.000 | 128.000 | 3.000 |
| PHI1 | 479.400 | 220.800 | 2.171 |
| GAMMA1 | −.039 | .020 | 1.980 |
| PSI1 | .270 | .404 | .667 |
| LY1** | 1.000 | | |
| LY2 | .641 | .296 | 2.166 |
| LY3 | .298 | .195 | 1.528 |
| TE1 | 2.902 | .859 | 3.378 |
| TE2 | .394 | .184 | 2.143 |
| TE3 | .546 | .150 | 3.646 |
| LISREL Estimates, N = 31 | | | |

*See Figure 3.3 for structure of model. (Adapted from Weber, 1984a, with permission of the Austrian Academy of Science.)
**Parameter fixed to 1 for purposes of identification.

reliable and valid. As predicted, this relationship is negative. The size of the coefficient (−.039) indicates that a 10 mark change in the rate of change of prices causes an increase (or decrease) of 4 wealth words per 1000. Because of the content-analytic procedures employed, it is likely that the size of the unstandardized coefficient understates the relationship between wealth-related issues and economic performance. The investigators counted only those words that by themselves indicate wealth concerns rather than total words in sentences dealing with economic problems. Had the latter been done, the size of the coefficient might be substantially higher because the variance of the dependent variable would be higher. It is also worth noting that if all the observed and latent variables had zero means and standard deviations of one, then the coefficient between economic performance and wealth concerns would be −.855, which is certainly a substantial relationship.[61]

## Concluding Remarks

The techniques presented in this chapter illustrate a range of possibilities for content analysis ranging from detailed analysis of word or phrase usage (KWIC lists and concordances) to multivariate analysis based on quantification. Other quantitative means of analysis were omitted because of space limitations. These include regression analysis and time-series regression models (Weber and Namenwirth, 1984a; forthcoming).

The spirit of the preceding presentation is illustrative and didactic. It is worth repeating that there is no single "right way" to do content analysis. Instead, each investigator must judge what methods are appropriate for her or his substantive problem. Given the ubiquity of computers, there is a real danger that as software for content analysis becomes more widely distributed, as the costs of encoding texts in machine-readable form continue to decline, and as the opportunity for capturing texts for analysis directly from other electronic mediums increases (e.g., newspaper editing and composing systems, word processors and typesetters, and newswires), the danger of mindless content analysis will also increase. One reason content analysis is not more widely utilized is that it is difficult and time-consuming to do well. Computers eliminate some of the drudgery, but time, effort, skill, and art are required to produce results, interpretations, and explanations that are valid and theoretically interesting.

The brief concluding chapter that follows addresses some of the likely developments of the next five years and the problems that must be resolved.

## Suggestions for Further Reading

Anyone contemplating doing content analysis would be well advised to look carefully at Stone et al. (1966). Rosengren (1981) presents several studies of the Swedish symbol system based on human-coded content analysis. The early classics of Lasswell (e.g., Lasswell et al., 1965; Lasswell et al., 1952) Pool (1951, 1952a, 1952b, 1959), and Berelson (1952) are still worthwhile reading to see what kind of problems they addressed and how they resolved them.

There is also a large "computers and the humanities" literature, including a journal by that title currently published by Paradigm Press. Papers from several conferences on computers and the humanities have also been published, including Wisbey (1971), Aitken et al. (1973), and Jones and Churchhouse (1976). A related text is Oakman (1980).

## 4. INTERPRETATION AND THE
## FUTURE OF CONTENT ANALYSIS

Exploring a variety of currently available techniques, the preceding discussion of content analysis has been fairly sanguine. However, this brief, concluding chapter notes some of the more difficult problems inherent in text analysis and suggests that computer systems now under development may resolve many of them in the next 5 to 10 years or so. Finally, this chapter discusses some recent advances in the realm of artificial intelligence that will become available in the future.

Irrespective of method, interpretation is an essential component of research. Data do not speak for themselves, but the researcher must explain their significance in light of theoretical and substantive concerns. On a particular problem, the researcher brings to bear a wide range of theoretical, methodological, and substantive knowledge. Content analysis is both interesting and difficult precisely because it explicates various problems of interpretation that are shared with other methodologies:

- What do the results mean?
- Are there competing interpretations?
- Does the interpretation of the results make sense in light of some theory or theories?
- How do we decide whether the interpretation is in some sense correct?

Analogous questions arise directly from the fact that the raw data are symbols. What do words or other semantic units mean to their author(s), their readers, and to the content analyst? How do we know this? Unfortunately, there are no simple answers. Also, diverse fields of inquiry, including semiotics, hermeneutics, linguistics, philosophy, cognitive science, and artificial intelligence address these problems differently.

The solution of many interpretation problems, especially as they pertain to automated content analysis, involves the knowledge required for interpretation and how humans and computers use it. One major advantage of computer-aided content analysis is that it must explicate the interpretive process, shedding light on problems common to all modes of interpretation. As an introduction to the current and future range of possibilities in computer-aided content analysis, this chapter discusses a few of the difficulties involved. For instance, some procedures require that the computer represent a great deal of knowledge although other procedures do not. In interpretation, there is also a difference between the kinds of knowledge required by humans and computers, and the needed interaction between human and computer knowledge poses further problems.

## Interpretive Problems in Content Analysis

Difficulties often arise because our quantitative measures are crude. They usually make broad rather than narrow distinctions. For theoretical or practical reasons it is often necessary that otherwise relevant linguistic information be ignored. Consequently, the interpretation of results is often not straightforward. A few examples will explain this point.

Ogilvie (1966) showed that even when one is looking at raw summary scores, extreme caution is always in order. Analyzing data for one participant in a small group that met together for several sessions, Ogilvie found that category summary scores suggested that the participant "Windle" was a person with "seething anger." Examination of retrievals from the text based on combinations of categories,[62] however, showed that this interpretation was incorrect. It revealed a person eager to please and to be accepted; in short, "Windle" proved to be a very "other directed" individual. Ogilvie's paper demonstrates that the careful investigator must move back and forth between the text and the output of the content analysis, progressively refining and validating hypotheses.[63]

The previous chapter noted that when content variables are subjected to statistical analysis, no one should accept the results at face value. For instance, when summary scores are factor analyzed, the results usually suggest the existence of themes in texts. A critical next step in the research process is to attempt to validate the interpretation of themes first derived from the statistical results. Validity can be confirmed or denied by returning to the original text to find examples of the hypothesized themes. This validation process is crucial. Investigators should never assume that the meaning or significance of quantitative output is so clear that face validity will suffice, and, consequently, that they do not have to return to the text.

Note that the investigator must relate theory, text, and the results of the content analysis procedures. This interpretive process entails the interaction among several bodies of knowledge, little of which is actually represented within the computer.

Even where our existing computer procedures can represent a little knowledge, how much information is necessary for the task at hand? Consider the following example.

As noted in Chapter 2, a central question in content analysis is whether the content classification is semantically valid; that is, do words or other recording units classified in the same category have some meaning in common? As we have seen, sometimes the answer to this question is not simple.

In the early and mid seventies, Stone and his collaborators (Kelly and Stone, 1975) developed an improved version of the General Inquirer computer system for content analysis. This system was discussed previously but this chapter briefly covers similar ground from a different perspective. The newer General Inquirer can differentiate among the various senses of homographs. For example, is the word "picture" a verb, noun, or part of a phrase indicating a kind of window? Is "find" a transitive or intransitive verb or a noun? Consider the word "state." The General Inquirer can differentiate seven different senses or uses:

- state (noun), body politic—area of government
- situation, such as "state of science"
- "to state" (verb), to declare
- "state of affairs" (idiom)—situation
- "united states" (idiom)—handled by "United"
- "ship of state" (idiom)—government, handled by "ship"

What kind of knowledge is required for this primitive disambiguation? The computer "knows" or has access to much information, one sentence at a time. It can differentiate words from punctuation. It knows where the beginning and end of each sentence are and what words precede and follow a word in question, such as "states." Also, it usually knows some of the syntactic and semantic characteristics of preceding and following words. The investigator can give the General Inquirer (or any comparable computer program) a set of rules for distinguishing various idioms and word senses.

For example, if the root "state" ends in -ed, or -ing, then the word must be the verb sense (stated or stating). If the preceding word is "united," then the rules for "united" will take care of the phrase "United

States." Stone's rules for "state" also take care of the phrase "state of affairs."

Obviously, this is an improvement because the precision of text classification is increased. But in fact, only a limited amount of information is given to the computer. Stone's disambiguation of "state" is itself a simplification. The *Random House Dictionary of the English Language* (college edition) lists 17 different senses for "state." The *Oxford English Dictionary* lists at least 41 different meanings. Obviously, for a particular investigation, not every shade of nuance will be important. In the interest of parsimony, 5, 7, or 10 senses may be quite sufficient. Clearly, the investigator chooses the number of distinctions on substantive grounds. For some purposes it may not matter if the finest possible distinctions are blurred. Furthermore, it does not make much sense to insist on linguistic distinctions that are not part of the distinctions made by the category scheme.

Does this increase in precision make any difference substantially? Perhaps it does. The most important contribution is that disambiguation greatly increases the validity of these and related modes of content analysis. Also, the ability to distinguish among the various senses of homographs forces the investigator to make more explicit and therefore perhaps better decisions about what kind of semantic differences are important in light of her or his substantive or theoretical concerns.

There is little doubt that this kind of primitive disambiguation is only a modest step. Chief among its practical advantages is that the technology that makes it possible is inexpensive. The computer can quickly process large amounts of text at nominal cost. However, experimental systems now being developed incorporate significant improvements in text understanding.

## Computational Hermeneutics

To show one current state-of-the-art approach to computer-based text analysis, this section presents brief excerpts from Dyer's (1983) book *In-Depth Understanding*. This work represents some of the research done on natural language understanding at the Yale Artificial Intelligence Laboratory. One goal of this research is to design a computer system that understands narrative in some sense. In this paradigm, understanding is achieved when the computer can correctly respond to questions concerning a particular narrative and can make correct inferences about matters implied, but not directly stated, in the narrative.

### BRIEF NARRATIVE—DIVORCE, PART 1

George was having lunch with another teacher and grading homework assignments when the waitress accidentally knocked a glass of Coke on him. George was very annoyed and left, refusing to pay the check. He decided to drive home to get out of his wet clothes.

### HUMAN QUESTIONS AND COMPUTER ANSWERS

Q: What did George do for a living?
A: GEORGE WAS A TEACHER.

Q: Where did George have lunch?
A: AT THE RESTAURANT.

Q: What happened at the restaurant?
A: THE WAITRESS SPILLED COKE ON GEORGE AND HE REFUSED TO PAY THE CHECK.

Q: How did the waitress feel at the restaurant?
A: THE WAITRESS REGRETTED THAT SHE SPILLED COKE ON GEORGE.

Q: Why did George go home?
A: GEORGE WANTED TO CHANGE HIS CLOTHES.

Q: How did George get home?
A: GEORGE DROVE.

### BRIEF NARRATIVE—DIVORCE, PART 2

When he got there, he found his wife Ann and another man in bed. George became extremely upset and felt like going out and getting plastered. At the bar he ran into an old college roommate, David, who he hadn't seen in years. David offered to buy him a few drinks and soon they were both pretty drunk. When George found out that David was a lawyer, he told him all about his troubles and asked David to represent him in court. Since David owed George money he had never returned, he felt obliged to help out.

### MORE QUESTIONS AND ANSWERS

Q: How did Ann feel when George caught her cheating on him?
A: SHE WAS SURPRISED.

Q: Why did George want to get drunk?
A: HE WAS UPSET BECAUSE HIS WIFE WAS CHEATING ON HIM.

Q: Who was David?
A: GEORGE'S COLLEGE ROOMMATE.

Q: What did David do for a living?
A: HE WAS A LAWYER.

Q: Did George borrow money from David?
A: NO. IT WASN'T GEORGE WHO BORROWED MONEY, IT WAS DAVID.

First, note that the narrative does not directly say that George is a teacher; this inference is made from the text. The computer is able to determine the referents of pronouns, something that is not possible with the techniques discussed earlier. The word "restaurant" is not mentioned either, but implied. Note also that the program attributes feelings to the waitress and takes motivations into account. The computer system can distinguish true from false, and therefore has some limited reasoning ability, as exhibited by the answer to the last question.

What are the kinds of knowledge required to understand such stories? Besides knowledge about language such as syntax, at least nine other domains of knowledge are represented within the computer system. These are:

- goals,
- plans for achieving goals,
- affect or emotions,
- events and scripts concerning events,
- interpersonal relations,
- social roles,
- reasoning and beliefs,
- settings, and
- abstract themes

A detailed discussion of Dyer's (1983) computer system is far beyond the scope of this chapter. However, computational hermeneutics will help explicate the interpretive process, with the likely consequence that all interpretation might benefit as the strengths and weaknesses of various formalisms are identified.

Although work such as Dyer's is meant to contribute to artificial intelligence (AI) and cognitive science, social science inquiry will also adapt it (and other advances in AI). Therefore, in the future, the ability of computer programs to understand text will permit the computer to identify similar themes in diverse texts, thus constituting a much more powerful and valid form of content analysis. The explanation of variation in themes over time or across sources is the remaining task. Alternatively, the analysis might take variation in themes as independent or intervening variables, examining changes in society, economy, or polity.

Two notes of caution are in order. Although AI research has made great progress, especially in the past five years, the field is still in its infancy (Winston, 1984). It is dangerous to expect too much too soon. Besides, these sophisticated procedures are much more costly than those described in previous chapters.[64] Several person-years of work went into the development of the system described in Dyer (1983). Unfortunately, it can understand only a very limited number of topics.

## Concluding Remarks

Techniques for computer text analysis and comprehension now being developed by AI researchers may provide the bridge (or link between) so-called qualitative and quantitative approaches to social science inquiry. For those who wish to count, AI formalisms may provide a clear and detailed account of the qualities to be counted. Such precision often has been lacking in the past.

The previous chapters showed a diverse set of somewhat limited content analysis procedures that are useful in social science research. Although this book has focused on method, the quality of the answers they provide to the substantive and theoretical questions will determine the ultimate worth of these techniques.

## Suggestions for Further Reading

For those without computer experience, Boden (1977) is an outstanding introduction to AI. She presents thorough descriptions of several key pieces of research at the intersection of AI and psychology. Winston (1984) presents some of the key AI ideas from a more diverse set of problems. Weizenbaum (1976) presents a more gloomy view of AI. Most AI programming is done in a language called LISP (Winston and Horn, 1984). Winograd (1983) and Brady and Berwick (1983) are recent contributions to the literature on natural language processing from an

AI perspective. Each has an extensive bibliography. Dyer (1983) and Carbonell (1981) represent some of the recent work done at Yale University.

# APPENDIX:

## COMPUTER SOFTWARE AND TEXT DATA ARCHIVES

TEXTPACK, a comprehensive software system for text analysis, is now being distributed for a nominal charge by the Computer Department/ ZUMA/ The Center for Surveys, Methods, and Analysis/ B 2, 1/ D-6800 Mannheim 1/ Federal Republic of Germany. Written in the FORTRAN77 computer language, this software will run on micros (e.g., APPLEs, IBM PC's), minis (e.g., DEC VAXs, PRIME computers), and larger mainframes (e.g., IBM) that have FORTRAN77 compilers. TEXTPACK documentation is available in either English or German.

As desired by the investigator, TEXTPACK V will perform or generate frequency counts of words, key-word-in-context (KWIC) lists, key-word-out-of-context (KWOC) lists, comparisons of vocabularies, cross-references, procedures for iterative dictionary construction, retrievals of text units, reduction of text via go-stop-lists, and tagging (OR-function for all systems, OR, AND, NOT, BEFORE, AFTER, NOT functions for IBM and Siemens versions). In addition, there are interfaces for the major statistical packages. However, full disambiguation is not available at this time.

The Oxford Concordance Program (Hockey and Marriott, 1982) is another widely distributed program that is often used for text analysis. Used mainly by those in the humanities, the OCP can be used to generate concordances, word frequency lists, and word indices (indicating the occurrence of all or selected words by line number) from texts in a variety of languages and alphabets. There is some evidence that TEXTPACK software runs faster than the OCP, and is therefore less expensive to use. However, interested readers can obtain OCP documentation and software for a modest fee from Oxford University Computing Service/ 13, Banbury Road/ Oxford, OX2 6NN/ England. The OCP is written in the older FORTRAN66. There do not appear to be any machine dependencies, but readers should check with Oxford before ordering.

The KWIC listings presented in this book were generated using the Key-Word-In-Context Bibliographic Indexing program (Popko, 1980). This software is written in PL1, and can be used on IBM computers that support the PL1 language. This version of KWIC can be obtained for a fee from the Laboratory for Computer Graphics and Spatial Analysis/ Graduate School of Design/ Gund Hall/ Harvard University/ Cambridge, MA 02138.

Software for text analysis is often described in the journal *Computers and the Humanities,* currently published by Paradigm Press, P.O. Box 1057, Osprey, FL 33559-1057.

Finally, many data base programs on micros and larger computers have some text analysis capabilities. Examples of these are given in Brent (1984).

At this writing, few text data sets have been archived and made publicly accessible. The ICPSR at the University of Michigan has at least two text data sets created by Holsti and North. One contains a sample of the replies to the British Speeches from the Throne given at the opening of each session of Parliament. Another file contains the speeches of the German kaiser. The latter data set was found to be incomplete and contains numerous errors. The former data set is poorly documented.

The entire texts of Democratic and Republican (Whig) Party platforms (1844-1964) have been archived at the Roper Center, University of Connecticut, Storrs, CT 06268. They are available on computer tape through the Roper center for a small fee. These data also are available in Europe from the Zentralarchiv Fur Empirische Sozialforschung/ Bachmer Strasse 40/ D-5000 Koln 31/ FRG. In addition, British Speeches from the Throne at the opening of Parliament, 1689-1972, will also be archived at the same institutions.

# NOTES

1. Various authors have proposed formal definitions of content analysis. For example, Stone et al. (1966: 5) state the following:

> Content analysis is any research technique for making inferences by systematically and objectively identifying specified characters within text.

Krippendorff (1980: 21) defines the method as follows:

> Content analysis is a research technique for making replicable and valid inferences from data to their context.

Krippendorf is right to emphasize the relationship between the content of texts and their institutional, societal, or cultural contexts. This issue is taken up in Chapter 3.

2. Other perspectives on text analysis include linguistics, pscyhology, and artificial intelligence, which is discussed in Chapter 4. As noted in Chapter 3, there is also a large "computers and the humanities" literature that partly overlaps the concerns of this monograph.

3. *Meaning* refers to shared as opposed to private undertandings.

4. Category names are capitalized throughout.

5. Another, more qualitative or clinical tradition of content analysis is not emphasized here. See, for example, George (1959a, 1959b), Berelson (1952: Chap. 3), and some of the articles in a special issue of *Qualitative Sociology,* 1984, vol. 17, numbers 1 and 2.

6. Various systems for computer-aided content analysis are more or less successful in distinguishing among various word meanings and connotations. This problem and several resolutions are discussed in later chapters.

7. If one of the measures has already been shown to be valid, the other must be valid also, unless some third, unincluded variable is responsible for the association among the first two. But multiple indicator models (Joreskog and Sorbom, 1979) do not require that one indicator be deemed valid a priori.

8. *Construct validity* has been used to refer to two different types of validity; hence there is some confusion over the term. Cook and Campbell (1979: 59) use the term to refer to "the possibility that the operations which are meant to represent a particular cause or effect construct can be construed in terms of more than one construct. . . ." Others, following Cronbach and Meehl (1955), use the term *construct validity* to refer to the fit between data and constructs suggested by theory. The present discussion uses the former definition, and following Brinberg and McGrath (1982), refers to the latter definition as *hypothesis validity,* which is discussed below.

9. This is what Janis (1965) refers to as *indirect* validation, which he suggests is the main form of validation for content analysis. However, hypothesis validity has an important weakness: If the relationship between a content and noncontent variable is counter to theory, does this invalidate the variables or the hypothesis?

10. There is nothing inherent in content analysis techniques to limit predictive validity; rather, investigators seldom include assessments of predictive validity in their research designs.

11. This form of coding is based on Osgood's (1959) Evaluation Assertion Analysis. Also see Holsti (1966, 1969). A more sophisticated form is used by Axelrod (1976) and his collaborators in the coding of cognitive maps of political elites. Appendix 1 in that volume gives detailed coding rules.

12. Holsti (1969: 104-116) gives numerous examples of broad and narrow category schemes for content analysis.

13. It is routine to tag 90%-95% of the words in most nonspecialized texts using general dictionaries. In addition, they can easily be modified to handle highly specialized texts, such as the speeches of the presidents of American scientific associations (Namenwirth, 1984b).

14. One reason content analysis did not blossom the way survey research did was that the lack of standardized procedures and measuring instruments worked against the accumulation of comparable results.

15. Many of the examples presented here are based on the General Inquirer system. At present, the TEXTPACK program mentioned in Appendix A will do everything that the General Inquirer can do, except disambiguation.

16. Table 2.1 is adapted from Namenwirth and Weber (1984) and Lasswell and Namenwirth (1968). Table 2.2 is adapted from Dunphy et al. (1974).

17. Current computer software can distinguish the various senses of words with more than one meaning, or homographs. This is discussed later in the chapter.

18. For example, low variance or oddly shaped distributions often cause problems in statistical estimation.

19. Distinctions may be also be syntactic, for example, identifying syntactic categories such as verbs, nouns, and modifiers. More precise classification results from correctly classifying modifiers, for example, into more specific classes, such as adjectives and adverbs.

20. TEXTPACK V also has some capabilities for dealing with idioms

21. Artificial intelligence (AI) techniques provide a proper solution to the problem, but the software and hardware required will not be widely available for some time. An example of AI software for natural language processing is discussed in Chapter 4. Hardware is mentioned in note 64.

22. For simplicity, this and the next table omit the syntactic and marker categories assigned to each word. The latter are used in the disambiguation rules, and are not normally used in substantive interpretations.

23. Except for subcategory/category-total assignments (e.g., Wealth-Other/Wealth-Total), the LVD is a single-classification dictionary. Words or word senses are assigned only to one substantive category. The Harvard IV is a multiple-classification dictionary in which word senses may be assigned to more than one substantive category.

24. Intensity might be taken into account by multivariate models such as factor analysis and multidimensional scaling. In that case intensity is indicated by magnitude of the factor loadings or MDS weights. See Weber (1983) for a more technical discussion.

25. Note "Weber's Paradox" (1983): Results using the Lasswell dictionary have not been interpreted or explained using Lasswell's theory, and results using the Harvard dictionary have not been interpreted or explained using Freudian or Parsonian theory. At present, general dictionaries should be considered useful, common-sense category schemes rather than the operationalization of a formal theory.

26. Krippendorff (1980: 157) distinguishes between "emic or indigenous rather than etic or imposed" categories, asserting without evidence that only the former are semantically valid. This raises sticky problems concerning both category schemes and manifest versus latent content. See Namenwirth and Weber (1984) for an extended discussion.

27. Factor analyzing word counts to infer themes has a long history, which is reviewed by Iker (1974). Stefflre's (1965) work makes an early programmatic statement. Moreover, each approach entails a different measurement model. Specifically, first-order exploratory factor analysis is the statistical model that corresponds to inferring themes from word covariation. The measurement model for single-classification-assumed dictionaries corresponds to a restricted second-order confirmatory factor analysis (Weber, 1983). I am unaware of any attempt to analyze the same texts using both measurement models. Therefore, it is uncertain whether these different approaches yield similar or different substantive findings.

28. Both the Harvard and Lasswell dictionaries emphasize institutional aspects of social life. In addition, Zvi Namenwirth played a large role in the creation of the Lasswell and early Harvard dictionaries. Therefore, some will not be surprised if his results do replicate across dictionaries.

29. Usually percentages or proportions are used to standardize for the length of the document or other unit of text. However, these create other problems for analysis, as mentioned in Chapter 3.

30. In choosing a simple random sample, each member of the universe or population to be sampled has an equal probability of being included in the sample.

31. In choosing a stratified random sample, each member of each subclass of the population has an equal probability of being included in the sample, but a different proportion of each subclass may be chosen. Put another way, the probability of a particular member of the population being chosen depends on which subclass that member belongs to.

32. Other optical scanners require that the text be prepared using special fonts, type balls, or daisy wheels.

33. Names and addresses of KDEM service bureaus can be obtained from Kurzweil Computer Products, 185 Albany St., Cambridge, MA 02139. At present, there are more than 20 such service bureaus.

34. The KDEM has a computer terminal for the operator. Characters that it cannot interpret are highlighted (brightened) on the screen, and the opeator can make corrections, if necessary.

35. When the meaning of a word changes over time, KWIC lists often indicate these changes. Usually this poses no problem, because new meanings frequently entail additional usages, such as the change from verb to noun, noun to adjective, and so on. As illustrated below, computers can distinguish the various senses of homographs. Consequently, changes in meaning can be taken into account.

36. This version of KWIC prints the key word with all or most of the sentence in which it appears. In principle, however, there is no limit other than utility on the size of the context provided. Similar listings can be obtained with TEXTPACK V and the OCP.

37. Depending upon the goals of the content analyst, other senses could be distinguished (see Chapter 4).

38. The utility of ordered word frequency lists was suggested by Ronald D. Brunner (personal communication). The number of words included in the table was determined by space limitations rather than substantive or methodological considerations.

39. Table 3.3 and 3.4 are edited output from the Key-Word-In-Context Bibliographic Indexing program (Popko, 1980) that runs on medium and large IBM computers. Similar output can be obtained from TEXTPACK and the OCP. See the Appendix for further information.

40. However, in studies of disputed authorship, these types of words have been found to discriminate between authors (Mosteller and Wallace, 1964).

41. A second assumption is that changes or differences in word frequencies reflect differential concerns. This is likely to be true for rank orders but not for absolute frequencies, as absolute frequencies are partly a function of document length.

42. Retrievals of all kinds can be done with data base systems that run on microcomputers, discussed in Brent (1984).

43. In the computers and humanities literature these are called *collocations* (e.g., Firth, 1957; Haskel, 1971; Berry-Rogghe, 1973; Geffroy et al., 1973).

44. Very long sentences were broken up. Plus signs indicate semicolons.

45. In this and the following section, I draw on a larger text data base consisting of Democratic and Republican party platforms, 1844-1980 (Johnson, 1979, 1982) developed in collaboration with J. Zvi Namenwirth. See the Appendix for information regarding archived text data.

46. For each party, the data were standardized to a mean of zero and a standard deviation of 1.0 in order to eliminate differences of scale in the figure.

47. These results replicate and extend some of Namenwirth's (1966b) findings for the period 1844-1964.

48. The rows of the data matrix are documents or other units of text and the columns are content category or word frequency counts; one could also produce "Q" factor analysis by transposing (reversing) the rows and columns.

49. The relative merits of these approaches have been discussed extensively elsewhere (Weber, 1983).

50. This is a modification of the Harvard III Psychosocial Dictionary documented in Stone et al. (1966: 169ff).

51. Some categories were eliminated because of low variance or because they did not discriminate between mass and elite papers.

52. Principal components analysis is often confused with true factor analysis. The former excludes unique variances, but retains common and error variances. True factor analysis excludes both unique and error variances. However, most, if not all factor analysis solutions do not produce unique factor scores; principal components analysis does (Kim and Mueller, 1978; Rummel, 1970).

53. Pronouns and ambiguous references were identified in the text.

54. These definitions are from Stone et al. (1966: 174-176). The remaining definitions are from Namenwirth (n.d.).

55. ANOVA is used in the analysis of categorical independent and continuous dependent variables (e.g., see Rosenthal and Rosnow, 1984).

56. There were three time period corresponding to June 25, 1950, to October 31, 1950 (the beginning of hostilities until the intervention of the Chinese); November 1, 1950, to July 7, 1951 (the Chinese intervention until the beginning of truce talks); and July 8, 1951, to August 11, 1953 (the onset of truce talks until 15 days after signing the truce agreement).

57. Principal components was used, which, as noted, excludes unique variances, but retains common and error variances (Kim and Mueller, 1978; Rummel, 1970).

58. One can calculate the reliability of factor scores obtained through principal components by calculating the Theta reliability coefficient (Armor, 1974).

59. The idea of acceleration or changes in the rate of change may not be intuitively obvious, and so a few examples may help to clarify the matter. For each year the acceleration (or deceleration) of the economy is derived from prices for three years. If wheat prices are 50, 65, and 55 marks per ton in 1871, 1872, and 1873, respectively, then for 1872 and 1873 the first differences are +15 and –10, respectively. The second difference for 1873 is –25 (–10 – +15). Hence concern with wealth in 1873 is likely to be somewhat higher than average. This is intuitively plausible because the economy was improving between 1871 and 1872 and declining between 1872 and 1873. Consider another series of prices: 50, 55, and 65. In this case the first differences are 5 and 10, and the second difference is +5. This would indicate that the economy is growing at an increasing rate of change, and hence one would expect that in the third year the level of wealth concerns would be lower than average.

60. Figure 3.3 presents the values of various coefficients and the symbols frequently used to represent them in LISREL models. These are as follows (see Joreskog and Sorbom, 1979 and Long, 1983a, 1983b for a technical discussion and more detailed explication):

(1) Lambda Y (LY): factor loadings of the observed Ys on the unobserved dependent variables;

(2) Lambda X (LX): factor loadings of the observed Xs on the unobserved independent variables;

(3) Theta Delta (TD): covariance matrix of the residuals or error term for the measurement model of the latent independent variables;

(4) Theta Epsilon (TE): covariance matrix of the residuals or error term for the measurement model of the latent independent variables;

(5) Beta (BE): causal coefficients among the dependent variables;

(6) Gamma (GA): causal coefficients linking dependent and independent variables;

(7) Phi (PH): covariance matrix of the latent independent variables; and,

(8) Psi (PS): covariance matrix of the residuals in the structural model.

61. However, using the data reported above, Jan-Bernd Lohmoller and Herman Wold (1984) estimated our model using two alternative procedures, canonical correlation and partial least squares "soft modelling" (Wold 1975, 1981). Using procedures that make weaker statistical assumptions, they found weaker relationships between economic performance and wealth concerns. We believe, however, that the stronger assumptions incorporated in the LISREL model are justifiable. In any event, our research is still in the exploratory phase, and irrespective of estimation technique, the hypothesized negative relationship between economic performance and wealth concerns is confirmed.

62. The technique was discussed in Chapter 3.

63. This paper should be carefully studied by anyone doing content analysis because it underscores the necessity for caution and care when interpreting content-analytic data.

64. For example, a lot of current AI research, but not that reported in Dyer (1983), is being done on LISP machines, which are expensive ($60,000) dedicated one-person work stations (such as those developed initially at MIT and now made by SYMBOLICS, INC.). It will probably take another five years or so for the cost of such hardware to decline significantly. However, an excellent implementation of Common Lisp, the new standard dialect, is available for the IBM PC from Gold Hill Computers, Inc., 163 Harvard Street, Cambridge, MA 02139. They also provide at no additional cost an outstanding tutorial based on Winston and Horn (1984) that includes examples of the kind of natural language processing found in many AI applications.

# REFERENCES

AITKEN, A. J., R. W. BAILEY, and N. HAMILTON-SMITH [eds.] (1973) The Computer and Literary Studies. Edinburgh: Edinburgh University Press.

ALTHAUSER, R. P. (1974) "Inferring validity from the multitrait-multimethod matrix: another assessment," in H. L. Costner (ed.) Sociological Methodology 1973-1974. San Francisco: Jossey-Bass.

ALWIN, D. F. (1974) "Approaches to the interpretation of relationships in the multitrait-multimethod matrix," in H. L. Costner (ed.) Sociological Methodology 1973-1974. San Francisco: Jossey-Bass.

ANDERSON, A. B. (1970) "Structure of semantic space," in E. F. Borgatta (ed.) Sociological Methodology 1970. San Francisco: Jossey-Bass.

ARIES, E. (1977) "Male-female interpersonal styles in all male, all female, and mixed groups," in Alice G. Sargent (ed.) Beyond Sex Roles. St. Paul, MN: West.

———(1973) "Interaction patterns and themes of male, female, and mixed groups," Ph.D. dissertation, Harvard University.

ARMOR, D. J. (1974) "Theta reliability and factor scaling," in H. L. Costner (ed.) Sociological Methodology 1973-1974. San Francisco: Jossey-Bass.

AXELROD, R. [Ed.] (1976) Structure of Decision: The Cognitive Maps of Political Elites. Princeton: Princeton University Press.

Ayer Directory of Publications (1983) Philadelphia: Ayer.

BERELSON, B. (1952) Content Analysis in Communications Research. New York: Free Press.

BERRY-ROGGHE, G.L.M. (1973) "Computation of collocations in lexical studies," in A. J. Aitken et al. (eds.) The Computer and Literary Studies. Edinburgh: Edinburgh University Press.

BLALOCK, H. M. [ed.] (1974) Measurement in the Social Sciences. Chicago: Aldine.

BODEN, M. (1977) Artificial Intelligence and Natural Man. New York: Basic.

BRADY, M. and R. C. BERWICK [eds.] (1983) Computational Models of Discourse. Cambridge: MIT Press.

BRENT, E. (1984) "Qualitative computing: approaches and issues." Qualitative Sociology 7 (1 & 2): 34-60.

BRINBERG, D. and L. H. KIDDER [eds.] (1982) Forms of Validity in Research. San Francisco: Jossey-Bass.

BRINBERG, D. and J. E. McGRATH (1982) "A network of validity concepts within the research process," in D. Brinberg and L. H. Kidder (eds.) Forms of Validity in Research. San Francisco: Jossey-Bass.

BRUNNER, R. D. (1984) The President's Annual Message. Discussion paper 8. Boulder: University of Colorado Center for Public Policy Research.

————(1983) Forecasting Growth Ideologies. Discussion Paper 7. Boulder: University of Colorado Center for Public Policy Research.

————and K. LIVORNESE (1982) Subjective Political Change: A Prospectus. Discussion paper 5. Boulder: University of Colorado Center for Public Research.

BURNHAM, W. D. (1970) Critical Elections and the Mainsprings of American Politics. New York: Norton.

BURTON, D. M. (1982) "Automated concordances and word-indexes: machine decisions and editorial revisions." Computers and the Humanities 16: 195-218.

————(1981) "Automated concordances and word-indexes: the process, the programs, and the products." Computers and the Humanities 15: 139-154.

CAMPBELL, D. T. and D. W. FISKE (1959) "Convergent and discriminant validation by the multitrait-multimethod matrix." Psychological Bulletin 56: 81-105.

CAMPBELL, D. T. and E. J. O'CONNELL (1982) "Methods as diluting trait relationships rather than adding irrelevant systematic variance," In D. Brinberg and L. H. Kidder (eds.) Forms of Validity in Research. San Francisco: Jossey-Bass.

CAMPBELL, D. T. and J. C. STANLEY (1963) Experimental and Quasi-Experimental Designs for Research. Chicago: Rand McNally.

CARMINES, E. G. and R. A. ZELLER (1982) Reliability and Validity Assessment. Beverly Hills, CA: Sage.

CARBONELL, J. G. (1981) Subjective Understanding: Computer Models of Belief Systems. Ann Arbor: University of Michigan Research Press.

CLEVELAND, C., D. McTAVISH, and E. PIRRO (1974) "Quester-contextual content analysis methodology." Paper presented at the 1974 Pisa Conference on Content Analysis.

COOK, T. D. and D. T. CAMPBELL (1979) Quasi-Experimentation: Design & Analysis for Field Settings. Chicago: Rand McNally.

CRONBACH, L. J. and P. E. MEEHL (1955) "Construct validity in psychological tests." Psychological Bulletin 52: 281-302.

DEWEESE, L. C. III (1977) "Computer content analysis of 'day-old' newspapers: a feasibility study." Public Opinion Quarterly 41: 91-94.

————(1976) "Computer content analysis of printed media: a limited feasibility study." Public Opinion Quarterly 40: 92-100.

DUNPHY, D. C., C. G. BULLARD, and E.E.M. CROSSING (1974) "Validation of the General Inquirer Harvard IV Dictionary." Paper presented at the 1974 Pisa Conference on Content Analysis.

DYER, M. G. (1983) In-Depth Understanding: A Computer Model of Integrated Processing of Narrative Comprehension. Cambridge: MIT Press.

FIRTH, J. R. (1957) "Modes of meaning," in Papers in Linguistics 1934-51. London: Oxford University Press.

FISKE, D. W. (1982) "Convergent-discriminant validation in measurements and research strategies," pp. 72-92 in D. Brinberg and L. H. Kidder (eds.) Forms of Validation in Research. San Francisco: Jossey-Bass.

GEFFROY, A., P. LAFON, G. SEIDEL, and M. TOURNIER (1973) "Lexicometric analysis of co-occurrences," in A. J. Aitken et al. (eds.) The Computer and Literary Studies. Edinburgh: Edinburgh University Press.

GEORGE, A. L. (1959a) Propaganda Analysis. Evanston, IL: Row, Peterson.

——(1959b) "Quantitative and qualitative approaches to content analysis," in I.D.S. Pool (ed.) Trends in Content Analysis. Urbana: University of Illinois Press.

GERBNER, G., O. R. HOLSTI, K. KRIPPENDORFF, W. PAISLEY, and P. J. STONE [eds.] (1969) The Analysis of Communication Content. New York: John Wiley.

GREY, A., D. KAPLAN, and H. D. LASSWELL (1965) "Recording and context units—four ways of coding editorial content," in H. D. Lasswell et al. (eds.). Language of Politics. Cambridge: MIT Press.

HASKEL, P. J. (1971) "Collocations as a measure of stylistic variety," in R. A. Wisbey (ed.). The Computer in Literary and Linguistic Research. Cambridge: Cambridge University Press.

HOCKEY, S. and I. MARRIOTT (1982) Oxford Concordance Program Version 1.0 Users' Manual. Oxford: Oxford University Computing Service.

HOLSTI, O. R. (1969) Content Analysis for the Social Sciences and Humanities. Reading, MA: Addison-Wesley.

——(1966) "External conflict and internal consensus: the Sino-Soviet case," in P. J. Stone et al. (eds.) The General Inquirer: A Computer Approach to Content Analysis. Cambridge: MIT Press.

IKER, H. P. (1974) "An historical note on the use of word-frequency contiguities in content analysis." Computers and the Humanities 8: 93-98.

——and N. I. HARWAY (1969) "A computer systems approach to the recognition and analysis of content," in G. Gerbner et al. (eds.) The Analysis of Communication Content. New York: John Wiley.

——(1965) "A computer approach toward the analysis of content." Behavioral Science 10: 173-183.

JOHNSON, D. B. (1982) National Party Platforms of 1980. Urbana: University of Illinois Press.

——(1979) National Party Platforms 1840-1976 (2 vols.) Urbana: University of Illinois Press.

JONES, A. and R. F. CHURCHHOUSE [eds.] (1976) The Computer in Literary and Linguistic Studies. Cardiff: University of Wales Press.

JORESKOG, K. G. and D. SORBOM (1984) LISREL VI (Analysis of Linear Structural Relationships by the Method of Maximum Likelihood) Users Guide. Mooresville, IN: Scientific Software, Inc.

——(1979) Advances in Factor Analysis and Structural Equation Models. Cambridge: Abt Asociates.

KAPLAN, A. (1964) The Conduct of Inquiry. San Francisco: Chandler.

KELLY, E. F. and P. J. STONE (1975) Computer Recognition of English Word Senses. Amsterdam: North Holland.

KIM, J - O and C. W. MUELLER (1978) Factor Analysis: Statistical Methods and Practical Issues. Beverly Hills, CA: Sage.

KLINGEMANN, H. D., P. P. MOHLER, and R. P. WEBER (in progress) "The wealth theme in the speeches of the kaiser and economic change 1871-1912."

——(1982) "Cultural indicators based on content analysis." Quality and Quantity 16: 1-18.

KRIPPENDORFF, K. (1980) Content Analysis: An Introduction to its Methodology. Beverly Hills, CA: Sage.

LASSWELL, H. D. and A. KAPLAN (1950) Power and Society: A Framework for Political Inquiry. New Haven, CT: Yale University Press.

LASSWELL, H. D., N. LEITES, and Associates [eds.] (1965) Language of Politics. Cambridge: MIT Press.

LASSWELL, H. D., D. LERNER, and I.D.S. POOL (1952) The Comparative Study of Symbols. Stanford, CA: Stanford University Press.

LASSWELL, H. D. and J. Z. NAMENWIRTH (1968) The Lasswell Value Dictionary (3 vols.). New Haven: Yale University. (mimeo)

LOHMOLLER, J.-B. and H. WOLD (1984) "Introduction to PLS estimation of path models with latent variables including some recent developments on mixed scale variables," in G. Melischek et al. (eds.) Cultural Indicators: An International Symposium. Vienna: Austrian Academy of Science.

LONG, J. S. (1983a) Confirmatory Factor Analysis: A Preface to LISREL. Beverly Hills, CA: Sage.

————(1983b) Covariance Structure Models: An Introduction to LISREL. Beverly Hills, CA: Sage.

LORD, F. M. and M. R. NOVICK (1968) The Statistical Analysis of Mental Test Scores. Reading, MA: Addison-Wesley.

MARKOFF, J., G. SHAPIRO, and S. WEITMAN (1974) "Toward the integration of content analysis and general methodology," in D. R. Heise (ed.) Sociological Methodology, 1975. San Francisco: Jossey-Bass.

MELISCHEK, G., K. D. ROSENGREN, and J. STAPPERS [eds.] (1984) Cultural Indicators. Vienna: Austrian Academy of Sciences.

MERRITT, R. L. (1966) Symbols of American Community 1735-1775. New Haven: Yale University Press.

MOSTELLER, F. and D. L. WALLACE (1964) Inference and Disputed Authorship: The Federalist. Reading, MA: Addison-Wesley.

NAMENWIRTH, J. Z. (1984a) "Why cultural indicators?" in G. Melischek et al. (eds.) Cultural Indicators. Vienna: Austrian Academy of Sciences.

————(1984b) "Value change and contrasts in communities of scientists, chemists, and economists since 1900," in J. Z. Namenwirth and R. P. Weber (eds.) Culture Indicators Research: A Content Analytic Perspective. (manuscript)

————(1973) "The wheels of time and the interdependence of value change." Journal of Interdisciplinary History 3: 649-683.

————(1970) "Prestige newspapers and the assessment of elite opinions." Journalism Quarterly 47: 318-323.

————(1969a) "Marks of distinction: a content analysis of British mass and prestige newspaper editorials," American Journal of Sociology 74: 343-360.

————(1969b) "Some and long and short term trends in one American political value," in G. Gerbner et al. (eds.) The Analysis of Communication Content. New York: John Wiley.

————(n.d.) "The Namenwirth Political Dictionary." (unpublished)

NAMENWIRTH, J. Z. and R. BIBEE (1975) "Speech codes in the press." Journal of Communication 25: 50-63.

NAMENWIRTH, J. Z. and H. D. LASSWELL (1970) The Changing Language of American Values: A Computer Study of Selected Party Platforms. Beverly Hills, CA: Sage.

NAMENWIRTH, J. Z. and R. P. WEBER [eds.] (1984) "The Lasswell Value Dictionary." in J. Z. Namenwirth and R. P. Weber (eds.) Culture Indicators Research: A Content Analytic Perspective. (manuscript)

———(1974) "The Lasswell Value Dictionary." Paper presented at the 1974 Pisa Conference on Content Analysis.

NORTH, R. C., O. R. HOLSTI, M. G. ZANINOVICH, and D. A. ZINNES (1963) Content Analysis: A Handbook with Applications for the Study of International Crises. Evanston, IL: Northwestern University Press.

OAKMAN, R. L. (1980) Computer Methods for Literary Research. Columbia: University of South Carolina Press.

OGILVIE, D. M. (1966) "Procedures for improving the interpretation of tag scores: the case of Windle," in P. J. Stone, et al. (eds.) The General Inquirer: A Computer Approach to Content Analysis. Cambridge: MIT Press.

———P. J. STONE, and E. F. KELLY (1980) "Computer-aided content analysis," in R. B. Smith and P. K. Manning (eds.) Handbook of Social Science Research Methods. New York: Irvington.

OGILVIE, D. M., P. J. STONE and E. S. SHNEIDMAN (1966) "Some characteristics of genuine versus simulated suicide notes," in P. J. Stone, et al. (ed.) The General Inquirer: A Computer Approach to Content Analysis. Cambridge: MIT Press.

OSGOOD, C. E. (1959) "The representation model and relevant research methods," pp. 33-88 in I.D.S. Pool (ed.) Trends in Content Analysis. Urbana, IL: University of Illinois Press.

OSGOOD, C. E., W. H. MAY, and M. S. MIRON (1975) Cross-Cultural Universals of Affective Meaning. Urbana: University of Illinois Press.

OSGOOD, C. E., G. J. SUCI, and P. H. TANNENBAUM (1957) The Measurement of Meaning. Urbana: University of Illinois Press.

POOL, I.D.S. [ed.] (1959) Trends in Content Analysis. Urbana: University of Illinois Press.

———(1952a) The "Prestige Papers": A Survey of Their Editorials. Stanford, CA: Stanford University Press.

———(1952b) Symbols of Democracy. Stanford, CA: Stanford University Press.

———(1951) Symbols of Internationalism. Stanford, CA: Stanford University Press.

POPKO, E. S. (1980) Key-Word-In-Context Bibliographic Indexing: Release 4.0 Users Manual. Cambridge: Harvard University, Laboratory for Computer Graphics and Spatial Analysis.

PRESTON, M. J. and S. S. COLEMAN (1978) "Some considerations concerning encoding and concording texts." Computers and the Humanities 12: 3-12.

ROSENGREN, K. E. [ed.] (1981) Advances in Content Analysis. Beverly Hills, CA: Sage.

ROSENTHAL, R. and R. L. ROSNOW (1984) Essentials of Behavioral Research: Methods and Data Analysis. New York: McGraw-Hill.

RUMMEL, R. J. (1970) Applied Factor Analysis. Evanston, IL: Northwestern University Press.

SARIS-GALLHOFER, I. N., W. E. SARIS, and E. L. MORTON (1978) "A validation study of Holsti's content analysis procedure." Quality and Quantity 12: 131-145.

SCHANK, R. C. and R. P. ABELSON (1977) Scripts, Plans, Goals, and Understanding. Hillsdale, NJ: Lawrence Erlbaum.

SNIDER, J. G. and OSGOOD, C. E. [eds.] (1969) Semantic Differential Technique: A Sourcebook. Chicago: Aldine.

STEFFLRE, V. (1965) "Simulation of people's behavior toward new objects and events." American Behavioral Scientist 8: 12-15.

STONE, P. J., D. C. DUNPHY, M. S. SMITH, and D. M. OGILIVIE (1969) The General Inquirer: A Computer Approach to Content Analysis. Cambridge: MIT Press.

TUFTE, E. R. (1978) Political Control of the Economy. Princeton, NJ: Princeton University Press.

WALKER, A. W. (1975) The Empirical Delineation of Two Musical Taste Cultures: A Content Analysis of Best-Selling Soul and Popular Recordings from 1962-1973. Ph.D. dissertation, New School for Social Research.

WEBB, E. J., D. T. CAMPBELL, R. D. SCHWARTZ, and L. SECHRIST (1966) Unobtrusive Measures: Nonreactive Research in the Social Sciences. Chicago: Rand McNally.

WEBER, R. P. (1984a) "Content analytic cultural indicators," in G. Melischek et al. (eds.) Cultural Indicators: An International Symposium. Vienna: Austrian Academy of Science.

———(1984b) "Content analysis: a short primer." Qualitative Sociology 7 (1 & 2): 126-147.

———(1983) "Measurement models for content analysis." Quality and Quantity 17: 127-149.

———(1982) "The long-term problem-solving dynamics of social systems." European Journal of Political Research 10: 387-405.

———(1981) "Society and economy in the Western world system." Social Forces 59: 1130-1148.

———and J. Z. NAMENWIRTH (forthcoming) "La mediacion cultural del funcionamiento economico como determinate en las elecciones presidenciales U.S.A., 1892-1964" ("The cultural mediation of economic performance as a determinant of presidential elections, 1892-1964"). Revista Internacional de Sociologia.

———(1984) "Political issues, economic performance, and presidential election outcomes, 1892-1964." Cambridge, MA. (unpublished manuscript)

WEIZENBAUM, J. (1976) Computer Power and Human Reason. San Francisco: W. H. Freeman.

WINOGRAD, T. (1983) Language as a Cognitive Process, vol. 1. Syntax. Reading, MA: Addison-Wesley.

WINSTON, P. H. (1984) Artificial Intelligence (2nd ed.) Reading, MA: Addison-Wesley.

———and B.K.P. HORN (1984) LISP (2nd ed.). Reading, MA: Addison-Wesley.

WISBEY, R. A. (1971) The Computer in Literary and Linguistic Research. Cambridge, Cambridge University Press.

WOLD, H. (1981) "Model construction and evaluation when theoretical knowledge is scarce: on the theory and application of Partial Least Squares," in J. Kmenta and J. Ramsey (eds.) Evaluation of Econometric Models. New York: Academic.

———(1975) "Soft modelling by latent variables: the non-linear iterative partial least squares (NIPALS) approach," in J. Gani (ed.) Perspectives in Probability and Statistics: Papers in Honour of M. S. Bartlett. London: Academic.

ZELLER, R. A. and E. G. CARMINES (1980) Measurement in the Social Sciences. Cambridge: Cambridge University Press.

ROBERT PHILIP WEBER *is currently Statistical Consultant at the Office for Information Technology, Harvard University. He holds a Ph.D. in political sociology. His current research interests include adapting artificial intelligence techniques to model political belief systems and to analyze political documents. The author of several papers ananlyzing long-term social, economic, political, and cultural change, Dr. Weber is also finishing a book co-authored with J. Zvi Namenwirth, called* Culture Indicators Research: A Content-Analytic Perspective.